CLEFT TONGUE

CLEFT TONGUE
The Language of Psychic Structures

Dana Amir

Translation from Hebrew: Mirjam Hadar

KARNAC

"Speak You Too" from *Selected Poems and Prose of Paul Celan* by Paul Celan, translated by John Felstiner. Copyright © 2001 by John Felstiner. Used by permission of W. W. Norton & Company, Inc.

First published in Hebrew in 2013 as הפש מוהת by Magness Press, Jerusalem

First published in English in 2014 by
Karnac Books Ltd
118 Finchley Road
London NW3 5HT

British Library Cataloguing in Publication Data

A C.I.P. for this book is available from the British Library

ISBN-13: 978-1-78220-042-0

Typeset by V Publishing Solutions Pvt Ltd., Chennai, India

www.karnacbooks.com

To my children

CONTENTS

ABOUT THE AUTHOR

Dr Dana Amir is a clinical psychologist, training and supervising analyst at the Israel Psychoanalytic Society, poetess, and literature researcher. She is the author of four poetry books and two psychoanalytic non-fiction books. She is the winner of the Adler National Poetry Prize (1993), the Bahat Prize for Academic Original Book (2006), the Frances Tustin Memorial Prize (2011), the Prime-Minister Prize for Hebrew Writers (2012), the IPA Sacerdoti Prize (2013), and the Nathan Alterman poetry prize (2013). *Cleft Tongue,* her second non-fiction book, has recently received the Israel Science Foundation Grant. Dana Amir's papers were published in psychoanalytic journals and presented at national and international conferences. She is a lecturer at the university of Haifa and practices psychotherapy and psychoanalysis.

INTRODUCTION

This book is an attempt to think through psychic language, in its diverse forms and modes of expression, both within psychic structures as well as the inter-personal realm.

What kind of rupture does psychotic language create? What is an autistic syntax? What are the body's forms of expression and how do they render themselves to interpretation?

These and other related questions have preoccupied me over the years—not only in my analytic work with patients, and in response to the singular types of discourse that emerged in the analytic relations, but also in my encounter with literary works and the unique syntaxes their discourse creates with the reader.

Wilfred Bion (1977a), in his paper on the caesura, argues that in order to hear what happens inside it, one has to listen beyond the sound of spoken words. The type of attention he proposes is very reminiscent of the kind of listening required to hear musical "overtones". This listening identifies something that is not only beyond tones but beyond tonality as such: it is located outside the music scale though it emerges from it and is related to it. This kind of attention picks up what is hidden inside tonality but lacking any formal representation. At stake here are the floating elements, those that use another frequency and hence also require a different mode of reception. It is the overtones of the various musical instruments that are responsible for their vocal and tonal singularity. In analytic listening, as in listening to music, the ear must attend closely to the distinctive, singular core. It is this type of listening that the present chapters, dealing with the diverse psychic idioms, address. My intention is not only to outline the dialectic far-end textures, that is, to describe the paradigmatic instances of each psychic category, but also to identify these typical syntactic zones in their simple, everyday manifestations in ordinary language and in the non-pathological personality. The fact that this book focuses on apparently pathological structures (psychosis, perversion, autism and psychosomatic phenomena) is the outcome of my attempt to understand how the psyche creates itself through these structures, using them to constitute its own internal grammar.

The first chapter looks at two basic forms of delay in the development of psychic language, each of which can be associated with a different discourse: concrete language, which is based on flattening, and pseudo-language, which is rooted in concealment. The second chapter is devoted to the split between voice and meaning which marks psychotic syntax, as well as the latter's double function in defending the self against intolerable contact with an unconscious death wish. The subject of the third chapter is the chameleon language of perversion and the relationship between the perverse structure and the primal scene imagined as an empty event. This chapter is followed by one that suggests thinking of autistic syntax as an inverse use of the psychic musical "organ point". The fifth chapter discusses the language of trauma and its main characteristic, namely the absent function of the "inner witness". The sixth chapter discusses psychosomatic language through the distinction between metaphorical, metonymical, and psychotic bodily expressions. The final chapter is dedicated to the singular ethics of interpretation.

The various chapters include clinical illustrations as well as readings of literary works by Rilke, Beckett, Sartre, Brodsky, and Celan.

"By its sense of light, you divine the soul", writes Celan in his poem "Language mesh" (1959). This book is an attempt to illuminate the language's sense of light. If space, by its very nature, marks what is absent from it—then language, whose words are the openings in the mesh through which seeps the unrepresentable, is the closest we can get to what dwells beyond this representation as well as beyond any ability to represent.

CHAPTER ONE

From mother-tongue to language*

Language and melancholy

Language is first and foremost a depressive achievement involving both the concession of what cannot be articulated—and the giving up of the symbiosis with the other by acknowledging him or her as a distinct subject. Indeed, acknowledging separation is simultaneously the driving motivation to speak as well as an essential condition for establishing language.

J. -B. Pontalis, dealing with the relationship between language and melancholy, writes:

> Language is not a grip. It grasps nothing of the substance of the real, not even the minutest sample. [...] But neither is it a concession; it will not concede: 'that's not for me'. Of its very nature, it walks toward that which it is not. Since born of loss and having nothing of its own, its appetite is enormous! In order to live, it

---

*This chapter is based on the paper: Amir, D. (2010). From mother-tongue to language. *The Psychoanalytic Review*, 97(4): 651–672. Copyright: Guilford Press. Reprinted with permission of The Guilford Press.

can—indeed must—'incorporate' all, up to the body and beyond it: it is more alluring than genitals, more moving than tears, more convincing than a fist punch, it wounds, anaesthetises, stupefies … It has all the powers. In this motion which carries it from control and magic toward the consciousness of its essential emptiness, it oscillates between manic victory and melancholy. But while melancholy uncovers its nature—mania uncovers nothing but its effort. (Pontalis, 1980, p. 251)

And later in that same essay:

Language is simultaneously mourning made real and unending. What does the 'there is nothing to say' denote but the stupefied, stubborn refusal of that same *trauerarbeit* into whose hands the 'lost object', the 'nameless thing' and the 'sentence-less truth' delivers us? (Ibid. p. 252)

And finally:

A language that ignores the loss that creates and animates it, a language convinced that it proclaims truth, will not turn but on itself. (Ibid. p. 252)

In other words, language does not signify entities but rather that which cannot be attained. It is never "the thing itself", but rather a space created around that which it signifies. In this respect, it does not uncover the very being of what it tries to articulate, but rather testifies to its own incapacity to accede reality.

The capacity to establish language is conditioned both upon individuation and upon the ability to grieve. Indeed, establishing language enacts a similar ambivalence to that which takes place in the process of mourning, as it implies both an adherence to the object as well as the capacity to let it go and recreate it within. Once individuation is experienced as insufferable, so does the creation of language. Not only because the psyche refuses to give up the omnipotent illusion that the other inhabits within—an illusion which negates the need to speak—but also because speech itself demands separation: it assumes the very capacity to abstract the object from the concrete objective world of senses, creating a substitutive world of signifiers.

"Upon losing mother and relying on negation, I retrieve her as a sign, an image, a word", writes Julia Kristeva in a chapter of her book *Black Sun* entitled "The omnipotent meaning" (Kristeva, 1987a, p. 63). In *New Maladies of the Soul* she describes a patient who uses language as armour to protect himself from her presence and interventions. As a child who went unseen by his mother—he now goes on not seeing her. He calls his mother "the mother", rather than "my mother", to avoid contact with his suppressed intimacy with her (Kristeva, 1995, p. 11). His discourse is altogether abstract—thus keeping his self completely isolated. That way, the patient creates an "artificial discourse" based on logical and syntactical rules rather than on his own feelings and urges, bringing about a fissure between the discourse's symbolic function and the concealed regions of his non-spoken drives, a fissure that manifests itself through somatic symptoms. Instead of constituting an identity, his alienation from his body creates a self sufficient totality that misses nothing, and therefore needs no one (Kristeva, 1995, p. 14).

What are the conditions necessary for the creation of a living language? A language which gives the interior a sense of measure but also maintains its quest after immortality; its transcendental, godlike features; its prayer, its cry? A language that is capable of transcending itself as well as of observing itself, one that enacts truth rather than just describing it?

A discussion of the attacks on the creation of psychic language cannot bypass the question of the "mother-tongue"[1] and its significance and influence on the child's ability to constitute his or her own language. Does the mother-tongue constitute an emotional language that enables us to know and bear the insufferable, or does it haunt it, alienating itself from it? Does the mother welcome her infant's investigating gaze, or rather attack it and move it away?

There are various ways of negating language, two of them will be the focus of this chapter (and some of their variations will also appear throughout the next chapters): the first is the emptying of the object from the desire; the second is the emptying of the desire from the object.

In the first instance, which I call "concrete language", a psychic discourse becomes impossible. In the second instance, which I call "pseudo-language", the psychic discourse remains barren and empty, high brow, and false. In both cases, the lack of emotional authentic language is the enactment of an unbearable primary bond.

Kristeva writes:

> The child refuses separation and mourning and, instead of tackling the depressive position and language, takes refuge in a passive position, in fact a schizo-paranoid one dominated by projective identification. The refusal to speak that underlies a number of language-retardations is in fact an assertion of omnipotence and thus of primary ascendancy over the object. (Kristeva, 1987a, p. 63)

The lack of language in the two instances suggested above is indeed not evidence of the "melancholy of language", but rather a rejection of it. It creates an omnipotent language which is free from the confrontation with its agony. Neither concrete language nor pseudo-language develop via working through loss, but rather swing between an omnipotent pretension of creation—and a destructive urge (not less omnipotent though) to regress into primordial chaos.

Rethinking language

Current attachment theory moves away from the model where an early relationship is seen as generating a template for later relationships. Instead, it suggests that early experience, via its impact upon development at both psychological and neuropsychological levels, determines the "depth" to which the external environment may be processed. Suboptimal early experiences of care affect later development by undermining the individual's capacity to interpret information concerning mental states (Fonagy, 2001). The securely attached child perceives in the caregiver's reflective stance an image of him or herself as desiring and believing. The infant sees that the caregiver represents him as an intentional being and is able thus to internalise this representation in order to form his own sense of self. If the caregiver's reflective capacity has enabled her to picture the child's intentional stance in an accurate manner, then the child will have the opportunity to find himself in the other as a mentalising individual. At the core of our selves is the representation of how we were seen (Fonagy, 2001), or what Sullivan (1953) refers to as "reflected appraisals".

In situations where parenting is primarily pathogenic there develops a lack of an infant-attuned emotional-intentional mirroring environment that is necessary for the establishment of secondary representations for the infant's self-states. Without such secondary representations, the affective impulses of the "constitutional self" remain relatively inaccessible and non-conscious, resulting in feelings of emptiness and disorganisation and a deficient ability for impulse control (Fonagy, 2001). These infants are internalising reflections from the mother that are contaminated by her struggles with her own unbearable feelings, rather than reflections of the mother's comprehension of the infant's internal states. The mother's failure to utilise mentalization and operate from a capacity for reflective self-function impairs her ability to foster such developmental building blocks for her child (Fonagy, 2002).

Dealing with the impaired capacity for mentalization, Bion speaks of the isolating attack on the connection between psychic objects (such as thoughts or affects) and words, ultimately, as an attack on the internal combined parental couple and on the primal scene (Bion, 1957, 1959). Individual language, which gains its essential characteristics from the connection between a linguistic content and an emotional one, will often seem dead when this connection is not available or is forbidden.

From a different point of view, Britton (1993) sees the severed connection between experience and meaning as a pathological splitting, in which the child's strong wish for the mother's presence and function comes into conflict with the experience of a disturbed relationship. This conflict is then resolved by splitting the mother image into "a mother as presence" and "a mother as function". It is an arbitrary splitting which is aimed at preserving the representation of the good object and keeping it apart from the bad one.

Bollas (1989, 1993) has maintained that the infant learns "the grammar of its being" before learning the rules of language. But in what ways does that grammar of being affect "the grammar of language"? Furthermore, what are the relations between the early grammar of being and the ability to establish a psychic grammar, or psychic syntax, at all?

Three essential functions of the mother-tongue

Following these questions, I would like to suggest three essential functions of early motherhood which enable the child to establish an individual language.

The first function relates to the primary role of the mother-tongue as a non-persecutory context that dilutes the objects' threatening being (whether they are concrete objects or objects of thought), therefore enabling their naming as well as their linkage to other objects.

The second function has to do with the mother endowing the child with his or her proper name. Being the one who gives the child a proper name, she also has the power to desecrate that name's singularity, thus turning the very act of naming into an attack on speech.

The third function relates to the mother-tongue's willingness to present the father as a non-traumatic object, thus enabling his presence to erect a buffer between private and public and to enable the shift from singular to plural language. This is the shift from the first-person to the third-person of experience, which allows language to transcend the concrete sensual-emotional data and reflect upon it, namely rephrasing it in a common language that may be shared with others.

The influence of these three functions on the creation of concrete *vs.* pseudo-language will be now thoroughly discussed.

The first function, as described, is related to the non-threatening presence of the mother-tongue. The emotional mother-tongue is the context within which a text can be established, the context within which language can be formed. When the maternal context serves to dilute internal threats, then objects become unambiguous and name-able. Since an ambiguous object can never be given one name—only the steady validity of objects, as well as their benevolence, may enable the act of naming and linking. When maternal presence is non-threatening, the mother-tongue infuses the surrounding objects with her presence, creating a non-persecutory substratum which enables the child's willingness to touch them, to join them by thought, to believe that linkage between objects is indeed possible without one annihilating the other. But if the mother-tongue's presence is threatening, the child's basic curiosity might be ruined, as if a hollowed substratum were constituted, one upon which no eagerness *to know* could be formed. Curiosity always constitutes a wish to link. Where linking itself is experienced as an attack—curiosity might not develop at all.

In what way, then, is this first function connected to the establishment of concrete or pseudo-language? In the case of concrete language we can imagine a mother-tongue who was willing to name objects but not feelings, shedding light upon the external world but neglecting the internal one, who was present "as function" but not "as meaning" (Britton, 1993). Pseudo-language, on the other hand, testifies to a delusive maternal tongue, one which used language in order to distance the child from truth, using words as a means to conceal and to obscure and not as a means to uncover and to shed light. Where a pseudo-language is involved we can imagine a mother-tongue which filled the threatening silence not in order to calm the child's fears but in order to conceal those voices which might be exposed within it; a mother-tongue who was unable to give any object a stable and an unambiguous status, and within which objects kept on changing, evasive and misleading; A mother-tongue which itself was internalised as an evasive, unstable and threatening object.

The second function is connected to the mother-tongue as the one which gives the child his or her first name but might as well desecrate the singularity of that name, thereby turning the very act of naming into an attack upon the sensual-data, or upon what the child experiences as "the thing in itself". By "desecrating" I refer to a mother-child dyad where the mother is experienced as an omniscient object that does not allow the child his or her necessary hermetic space of thinking. When the child's thinking space is experienced as a shop-window, transparent and penetrable, rather than as a closed room, the child is not allowed to exist as a separated thinking subject. Being the first gift given to us by an-other—a name is also the first symbol of otherness. When the very singularity of a name is desecrated then the urge to establish a language of names is transformed into an urge to reject naming and hence to abstain from speech.

The third function points to the father's presence as erecting a buffer between private and public spheres. The father's presence actually conditions the transition to the "experience in third-person" (which enables one to reflect upon it) without dissolving "speech in first-person". In other words, it enables the child's safe transition to what Aulagnier called the "discourse of others" (Aulagnier, 2001), a discourse that responds to logical and cognitive common rules. Since any shift from private to common language might also involve a threat to singularity, only a non-violent father figure would enable a free flow between the singular and common registers of speech in a way that serves the child's authentic needs. When the mother-tongue presents the father's figure as traumatic, the shift from individual to common language might be damaged. In this case the individual might lock him or herself within his or her own private language until it becomes a non-communicative hermetic unit, or else renounce it altogether, completely adopting "common speech" and thus generating a pseudo-language.

What is a pseudo-language? It is a language that is too prone to generalisations, one which makes comparisons rather than differentiations, and that evades the private by rejecting any exception to the rule. This kind of language—which rejects exceptions—is a language that never transforms into a singular language. The shift from individual to common language corresponds to the shift from first-person to third-person in emotional speech. While the first-person sticks to the experience itself, without the ability to observe it from afar, the use of the third-person involves the capacity to observe oneself in a reflexive manner.

In *Tales of Love* (1987b) Julia Kristeva writes:

> It is in the eyes of a third party that the baby the mother speaks to—becomes a *he* [...]. Without the maternal 'diversion' towards a third party, the bodily exchange is abjection or devouring; the eventual schizophrenic, whether phobic or borderline, will keep its hot-iron brand against which his only recourse will be hatred. (Kristeva, 1987b, p. 34)

Without the ability to develop a speech of a third-person—the child would escape from his mother's love to hatred, the only limit he could possibly posit between "me" and "not-me", "him" and "not him". Pseudo-language is the only defence against that hatred as well as against madness.

Concrete vs. pseudo-language

While concrete language is a language that cannot create any link—pseudo-language is one that involves an alleged link. This is a language whose generalisations and plurality serve as an unconscious barrier between the speaker and his own singularity. A concrete language is created when the early mother-child unit is too empty, too emotionally hollow, and thus unable to constitute a substratum upon which the child can establish a private language or an experience of an "I". A pseudo-language is formed when the "private self" is violated, indeed desecrated. The result of such an early invasion is a defensive refusal of any private content, a refusal which finally leads the child to reject a language that would be in touch with truth or express inner truth.

One can say that while concrete language concerns damage done to the two primary functions mentioned earlier, pseudo-language is connected with undermining the third function as well. When the primary link conceals a secret, the very act of sharing—and therefore the very transition to common language—is experienced as an unbearable threat. It is for this reason that the analysis of patients with concrete language would be considered as a "developmental" analysis whose aim lies in creating basic conditions for establishing language in general, while the analysis of patients with pseudo-language would involve deep interpretational work whose aim lies in re-creating conditions which enable contact between cognitive language and one's private emotional truth.

In the case of concrete language the first-person voice is absent. The "I"'s regarding stance is therefore neither that of a speaker nor that of a listener. A person with a concrete language does not view things from afar—but is assimilated in them. He does not smell, but rather becomes the smell. He is not hungry—he *is* hunger. His language—as a reflection of his inner experience—lacks an experience of an "I" that can own feelings and sensations.

In the case of pseudo-language the "I" is not absent but hidden, not only from the sight of the other but from the speaker's own eyes. The unconscious purpose of pseudo-language is to enable a speech which bears no experience; a type of communication that transmits no feelings. As a matter of fact, pseudo-language is the use of the third-person not as a means of observing oneself, but as a way of exceeding being oneself or avoiding staying within the very experience of the self.

Since language, as such, illuminates multiplicity and distinctness—within a symbiotic relationship there is no point in establishing it, as a conversation is neither needed nor possible. The establishment of a singular language threatens the fantasy of "two objects with one heart". One could say that the main function of the pseudo-language is exactly this: emptying language of its ability to illuminate distinctness. Blurring the limit between self and other is in the service of both the refusal to see the other as well as the refusal to see oneself. Where there is no distance from the other, the other cannot hurt, abandon or penetrate the private "I". Where there is no distance from truth, truth cannot be looked upon or confronted.

Pseudo-language is a parasitic language that uses the other yet does not converse with it; it "swallows" the other and its idiomatic qualities—but does not recognise it as a separate subject. Instead, it *becomes* that other, simultaneously effacing its otherness and subsuming it into itself.

This way of using the other is very different from that which I described earlier when dealing with the absence of the "I" in the case of the concrete language. While in concrete language we are dealing with the absence of an "I" that contains and owns experience—in pseudo-language we are dealing with an "I" that rejects those parts of experience that can relate to the truth one is unable to digest. It is not about an absent developmental function, but rather about a defensive mechanism. The "use of the other" would be thus very different from the use of the other in the projective identification mechanism: instead of depositing in the other those unbearable parts of oneself in order to receive them back—the person with pseudo-language would assimilate parts of the other into himself, thus using them as a surrogate to his own authentic contents or as a surrogate to his own authentic speaking self. The result would be a dead language, perfectly articulated but based upon artificial foundations. It would be a language one can use to speak—but not to converse with, one that would stick to logical, intellectual sequences, even to historical details—as long as they remain "history" rather than a genuine experience of "historicity".

Clinical illustration: concrete language

Twenty-seven-year-old John seeks psychotherapy following some distress he is unable to name. He is suffering from various somatic symptoms, including dyslexia, digestion problems, physical lugubriousness, psoriasis and stuttering.[2] He is also socially rejected and isolated. During psychotherapy, all attempts to get to know him are thwarted: he remembers nothing, has nothing that he wants to talk about, and is troubled mostly by concrete issues. He does not want me to talk to him; he asks me for names of physicians that might help him with his skin condition; he wants practical instructions on how to pass examinations; and he troubles me ceaselessly with telephone calls outside of session hours, always on technical questions.

Therapy does not establish a shared language; indeed, sometimes it feels like there is no common language at all. The concrete continuum of speech itself is fragmented: words are uttered, but do not cohere to experiences, and therefore fail to create meaning. John can say "my teeth chatter", but is unable to say "I'm cold". He is able to recount that his legs shook when a neighbour threatened to beat him, but is unable to say he was afraid. The language he employs is a completely concrete, non-reflexive one. It does not act to link, but to withhold a linkage. It seems to place unconnected objects side by side in an arbitrary array, without binding them with meaning or by any experience of "I-ness".

I find myself using a most simple language, afraid to go beyond his words, keeping my interferences at a descriptive level, far from any comprehension. Sometimes I feel I'm being "pushed" to become active, in a way I do not recognise from other psychotherapies. I find myself telling him that little children learn about themselves when someone endows their sensations with meaning; that he seems to be isolated like that little child who shivers with no one telling him that he is cold, who cries with no one telling him how tired or hungry he is. For the child he was, feelings stayed arbitrary and vague, kept attacking him while bearing no meaning, accompanied with no tools that could enable him to predict or to name them.

For a very long period I feel quite frustrated since my language does not seem to be one with which I can communicate with him. Only later I realise that what was repeated between us resembled his mother's experience of him at the beginning of his life: an awkward bizarre and demanding little baby, so hard to love.

At a certain phase, John uncovers old diaries his mother had written following his birth. It becomes apparent that she had fallen into a post-natal depression after giving birth and showed no interest in her baby, taking care of him only in a technical fashion. Her diaries are full of detailed entries on his weight gain, the food he consumed, the number of centimetres he had grown, but contain however not one reference to his personality or subjective being. Reading the diaries confirms what could only have been guessed at from the transference relationship. John had recreated within the relationship with me the primal pattern of relations with his mother. He is unable to relate to me emotionally since he cannot believe that I may have an emotional interest in him. For this reason he speaks to me only of mundane, physical issues, the only issues his mother had reacted to. Furthermore, since his mother showed no interest in his emotional being, he, too, shows no interest in it, or in that of anyone else's.

Rather than a refusal of memory, this technical, concrete reduction of the transference relationship was the only way John could remember at all. Since his childhood experiences had no clear-cut contours, but were rather a continued, ongoing traumatised condition, and since the primacy and character of these experiences did not allow them to undergo mental processing—they were not registered as memories, but rather as an existential pattern forcing John to re-enact it time and again within any kind of interaction he had with himself or with others.

Despite the pain concomitant to the psychic isolation he has sentenced himself to through this reduction—something in its re-enactment has created the artificial feeling of familiarity and comprehensibility that has compensated for the primal experience of being interior-less and meaningless.

A year later, there was a shift. One day John arrived very agitated, telling me that the roof of his house was leaking. He had been unable to sleep all night: walking in circles around the leaking area, and feeling that he was going out of his mind. I told him that perhaps he was not recounting an actual leaking roof, but was alluding to a psychic one. Perhaps something sealed off long ago has suddenly "sprung a leak". Perhaps his huge anxiety stemmed not from the outer flood, but from an inner one. He listened, very quietly, then suddenly burst out crying. Many months later he cited this moment as the moment we had struck an alliance of faith.

The fact that John developed complex somatic symptoms is connected primarily to the fact that there was no language other than the symptomatic body language. One can say that the emotional contents were foreclosed, leaving the body to exist as an autistic detached entity whose somatic speech replaced the psychic one. The meaningless experiences were evacuated through somatic mechanisms (diarrhoea, stuttering and psoriasis). Not ever being digested, they remained as sort of "foreign bodies" within the psyche.

Lacking any capacity to own his feelings and thoughts—John had never developed a coherent experience of selfhood. Since he never internalised a containing object—he continued to deal with every kind of stress through its physical evacuation, thus leaving himself locked within his own symptomatic language, isolated and starved. His external detachment disguised an inner space that was inhabited by horror, and surrounded by fragile and penetrable walls. Whenever he encountered a threat to his fixed, stable routine, John experienced the same primal dread of leaking, of being annihilated, of falling forever. In that sense it was very clear that his psychotic anxiety of the leak from the roof signified his anxiety of the possible leak from the un-enveloped, uncontained psychic space.

In this fragile moment my intervention suggested a bridge between the external and internal realms which were ultimately dissociated. Language ceased being concrete and began to echo internality. The pain which was displaced from the psychic body to the physical one broke back in, opening a possibility of establishing both a psychic language and a psychic space. In the next years the capacity to turn arbitrary events into meaningful ones was built step by step. The delicate yet stubborn work of embroidery, though full of moments of regression and despair, eventually succeeded to create an emotional language, with both volume and depth. Years later, when he himself became a father, John chose to raise his son in a foreign language, which was not his mother tongue. To him this choice was connected to the attempt to give his son a different language than the one he himself had as a child: an emotional, psychic language. Interestingly, this choice, besides its metaphoric glow, was quite concrete. John brought his son to our last meeting, saying that he pondered whether to bring me a book—but decided to bring me his baby instead. To my surprised look he answered: "This is the gift you gave me. This is the gift you deserve to get." I thought to myself that what he meant to say to me at that moment was that the language that I gave him was not a literary one (marked by the possibility of bringing me a book)—but rather a literal language, one that enables life, one that creates life.

Clinical illustration: pseudo-language

Twenty-four-year-old Anna seeks psychoanalysis following an episode of major depression that lasted six months. A delicate young woman, she appears as if made of porcelain. There is something at once oddly beautiful and terribly ugly in her that catches my eyes. It is as if one cannot alight on a single, coherent experience of her face, since something in it changes continually, fluttering and moving.

When she begins to speak I notice that the flutter that characterises her face also governs her voice. An ongoing "vibrato" accompanies every sound she utters, regardless of the content it embodies. There is a feeling of a rich, seething and bubbling inner world—but her outward discourse is disjointed and her oddly "high" spoken language seems a written rather than a spoken one.

She is the eldest of four siblings, the daughter of a felon father and a weak, dependent mother. Her young sister is diagnosed as schizophrenic. The father faces charges of having sexually abused the younger sister during one of her hospitalisations in a psychiatric hospital, but Anna tells of the fact that she was a silent witness to signs of a sexual rapport between the father and the sister also when they were little girls, signs that the mother refused to see.

As a child, her grades at school were so low as to raise concerns over possible retardation. Later, she had to struggle to matriculate and managed to get into university, although at great pains. I now understand that her learning disabilities were part of a larger hardship that has to do with the ability to combine objects, to feel curiosity, to create a continuum of language and memory.

In her first session, she reports constipation that sometimes lasts weeks, anxiety attacks followed by sudden lapses of sleep during the day, and hours of weakness that reach the point of her not being able to get out of bed. She complains of concentration problems, appetite losses and chronic thinness despite desperate attempts at weight gain.

At the same time that she seeks analysis, Anna also seeks neurological clarification for what she describes as deepening memory hardships—a consultation that reveals nothing. I say to her: "You tell me that something inside you attacks not just memories as such, but memory itself"; she tears over, and says that she has indeed "activated" mechanisms of forgetfulness, trying "to move forcefully memories away from her screen". I tell her that the forgetfulness she is employing is perhaps her way of telling herself: "this I must not remember".

During one of the first sessions, she tells me of a recurring nightmare she has had during the last two years: she is in her own room in her parents' house and a group of people, all well-known to her, push her into a corner. The room has one door leading to the inside of the house and another external door leading to the outer yard. She runs to that door and wrestles with it, only to find that it is locked. This is the recurring part of the dream. Each time she has it, she wakes up at this stage and discovers that she has walked in her sleep to the door and that the noise that woke her up was the noise she made while trying to unlock it.

But the dream she has had two days before our session had three distinct changes in it. The first was that I was there too, apparently as part of that group of well known people. The second was that, as opposed to her previous memories, she couldn't remember having been physically attacked, but knows she felt threatened. The third change was that when she woke up, she found herself not wrestling with the door as usual, but rather trying to climb the wall behind her bed, screaming "help, help", and waking up from the sound of her own voice.

I ask myself what is it that she cannot hear except through her own voice? I think of the changed patterns in her dream: the fact that I was there, the fact that she was not concretely surrounded but only "felt threatened", the fact that she was not banging at the door but instead climbing "the wall behind the bed" (the analytical couch?), calling out for help (instead of trying to physically unlock the door). What had previously taken place "concretely" in those dreams is now taking place within language. I wonder whether that points to the fact that she now posits the existence of someone outside herself, someone who might hear.

Throughout the analytic sessions, there is a jarring gap between the rich, complex discourse of dreams and the "reality discourse" within which she would describe a mundane, boring, emotionally barren existence. She can, for example, devote half a session to describing the most concrete details of her previous day: at what hour she woke up, what she wore, what she ate, whom she met on the street etc. It is all given in a highly sophisticated language, in a bewildering dryness and without differentiation between essence and periphery.

She talks about her years-long anxiety that she was indeed retarded, an anxiety habitually reasserted by her mother, who would tell her each time anew that she "wasn't what she thought she was".

Did the mother have an interest in keeping Anna "not thinking", maybe also "not seeing"? Did she have an interest in neutralising the only other witness to what may have taken place in that home?

Interwoven with the rise of these questions are severe anxiety attacks. Anna returns from sessions and falls asleep for many hours, waking with no memory of what happened prior to falling asleep. The sleeping spells are similar to "electrical shortages" or dissociative phenomena. I notice that each time signs of a memory surface, she suffers a paralysing anxiety. I get the feeling that her anxiety has a double role: experienced as an anxiety of death, it appears in reaction to signs of life; experienced as a signal that she is going to die, it in fact signifies that something in her begins to live. Anna tells that she had always had a degree of insensitivity to her own body, that she could withstand pain sometimes until it was almost too late. Once, she says, she broke a toenail and walked around for the entire day not noticing it. Only when she took off her shoe in the evening did she notice that it was filled with blood. I understand how critical it was for her to "not feel" the pain. To keep it hidden, even from herself.

During this period, she shares dozens of dreams in every session. At times I feel those dreams actually put a strain on analytic process; that they are "replacing" the manifest, concrete discourse which is perhaps experienced as more threatening. At other times I understand that there are linkages that can only take place when she is sound asleep, and which she serves to me without their having been passed through her awake consciousness, as if she were a messenger delivering her dream and not its owner.

In one of those dreams, she tries to use a stapler when droves of dead ants come out of it. In another, she opens her mouth and finds that it is full of rotten teeth which she then tries to extract. She tells me of the ants that used to live under the floorboards of her parents' house, and how she was always terrified they would climb onto her bed when she was sound asleep. We talk about the fear of what is hidden inside her and might overcome her when she is weak and defenceless; about the fear of "opening her mouth" during analysis and exposing what's rotten inside.

Around this period, she begins to talk about the "high language" which she has always employed. It can be comic or irritating, with such sentences as "I had sauntered, forlorn, to the bus stop" or "I was roused from my slumber at dawn", with no clear harmony between the concrete content and the literary idiom. Her style of speech is arrogant, indeed keeps its hearer at arm's length. For the first time I understand that language has acted as a sort of a "second skin" for her, insulating her within the family, but also protecting her from invasion. She says she "can't find a middle ground". Speaking "too high or too low", she can't find the "one place that is really hers". The night after this session, she dreams that I guide her to analysis through barbed wire fences. When we reach my clinic she finds her mother there, who tells her that she, too, is my patient.

I find myself thinking how much her mother-tongue attacks any possibility of her having a room of her own. Is that why she had to invent her own, other and distancing language?

The motion uncovered in this analysis from its very beginning was the motion between concealing to exposing. Between waking, daily life—the meagre and barren evidence of which was a series of details jumbled up in chronological order, facts written between her and me as if I were her daily calendar (not even her personal diary)—and the rich nightlife, full of dreams, where her greatest secrets and sorrows came to light. Pain bled inside; it could not have been testified to—nor given up on; a kind of double, diabolical contract—with no possibility of winning. Between the prohibition on being ill and the prohibition on being cured, analysis meandered as between two walls of a strait, the strongest force propelling Anna through it being the power of negation; the negation of being as the only way to be.

The negation of the body/psyche appeared in all possible forms of attack: from learning disabilities (as a form of attack on linking) through attacks on appetite, on sexuality, on wakefulness (through the recurring lapses of sleep), on bodily excretions (through constipation), on memory, on liveliness (through suicidal tendencies), on psychic life (through isolating it in dreams), on speech (through the use of a pseudo-language), and on analysis altogether.

Anna continually effaces our sessions out of two main motivations: the first has to do with the insufferable contents linked to the incest that took place at home and her being a silent witness to it, unable to "open her mouth"; the second linked to the feeling of liveliness, which emerged through the contact with these contents. Assigning meaning to her anxiety was simultaneously her greatest wish and her most insufferable anxiety, since as a result of it Anna felt alive; and as the one who failed to save her sister from psychic death—she punishes herself with a prohibition on life itself. The effacing, then, is a double one: of both content and form; of the renewed access to memories on the one hand, and of the access to the liveliness stored in those memories on the other.

One of the things I noticed was that as opposed to the anxiety attacks at the outset of analysis, which had effaced all prior content, leaving behind only an experience of emptiness and meaninglessness, the attacks that accompany the second year of analysis stop effacing the thoughts that preceded them. Thus, I understand that the anxiety was not just an outcome of insufferable memories, but an attack on memory and thought as such.

I contemplate Anna's sleep after sessions, hours of sleep that efface all that was felt or thought before them, and understand that it was not only her way of evacuating insufferable contents, but also her way of attacking any possibility of a link between her and her unbearable internal objects. If she doesn't remember what happened, she cannot connect anything. If she cannot tell me anything—she also prevents me from remembering her, or from remembering for her, as well as from returning it back to her in my own language, or as something that can be uttered in language at all.

A dynamic of feeding and starvation is continually activated between us: she "expels" the insufferable anxiety through sleep, but "re-digests" the expelled nourishment through dreaming. She "feeds" me with dreams, but "starves" me through the barren, waking discourse during entire sessions when she deals with reality to its minutia, perhaps as a way of attacking liveliness, perhaps as a way of shattering emotional phenomena into the tiniest pieces so that it would be completely un-linkable and un-repairable.

One can say that while Anna's sister—who was violated by the father and neglected by the mother—has totally renounced common language and did not succeed in developing any form of "discourse of others" but rather regressed to psychosis—Anna herself chose pseudo-language in order to protect herself from psychosis as well as from hatred. This pseudo-language enabled her not only to talk without uncovering herself but also to "exist without being" herself. All three functions of her mother-tongue were damaged: the first function, that of presenting a context in which objects would become non-attacking and nameable; the second function, that of creating a singular private space (for the mother let the father pervade the private space of both her daughters, and in this sense prevented them from any representation of privacy and singularity); and the third function, that of presenting the father as a non-traumatic object, enabling a non-traumatic passage from individual speech to common language.

Anna's "high" spoken language actually echoed the same catch her life was imprisoned in. Indeed, it would seem like she had no mundane practice of daily, living, spontaneous speech that creates an emotional field and responds to the emotional speech of an-other. The effacement of her mother-tongue, a language she experienced as silencing and sterilising, a language that was established on a prohibition of expressing truth and creating truthful linkages (interestingly, she described her mother's speech many times as "lacking a comprehensible syntax") has created a groundless, hollow, pseudo-literary language, which instead of acting as a vehicle of self-expression, behaved as a buffer between herself and her pain, or between her and her living "I".

From that which divulges her interior, language has become a means of exiling herself from that interior. Instead of a mediator, language has become a sealer. It created a bubble that defended her from pain but emptied her of all her life energy. In effect, she had put herself to death, or put herself to a deathlike-sleep inside that bubble, maintaining life-signs but bereft of all liveliness.

The greatest analytic danger was that analysis would establish the same pseudo-language, therefore becoming something that separates between Anna and herself instead of something that enables a link. Will analysis be able to create a new, living language? One within which emotions could be transmitted and processed? Will analysis be able to build a language that is in itself an emotional container and an appara-tus of meaning?

One day she told me, excitedly, about a dream she'd had. She was sit-ting in her old school class and the teacher asked the pupils: "What do we need language for? Why can't the spoken language be substituted for the language of drawing?" The teacher then went on to draw under each word the object it signified, creating a line to separate each word from the other, as if seeking to prove that words are not only uncon-nected but also unnecessary for expression. On her way out of class, Anna walked through a dark, "chaotic" forest filled with twisted trees. To find her way out of that forest, she started calling each tree by name. When we talk about the dream she says: "That's analysis for me: calling things by name."

In the first part of the dream, the teacher draws objects as substi-tutes for words. This can be seen as the limits of Anna's inner language, which lays objects without any ability to emotionally connect between them. This artificial-syntax language is a dead language: one that does not link objects but separates them from their essence as well as from their meaning. This was indeed the language Anna came to analysis with, employing a pseudo-syntax that covered for a rejection of any kind of linking, a refusal of any kind of psychic language.

The second part of the dream represents what the analytical proc-ess itself may have been for her: calling things by their name and thus endowing them with meaning, not just as a form of "path finding" but also as a way of creating a psychic continuum, one whose very exist-ence conditions the establishment of a psychic language at all.

Discussion

For the kind of patients described in this chapter, the very act of naming, perhaps like the very act of interpretation within the analytic process, is sometimes experienced as an incomparable violence, leaving them exposed and defenceless.

In *The Violence of Interpretation* (2001), Piera Aulagnier writes:

> The mother's words and deeds always anticipate what the infant may know of them, and if [...] the offer precedes demand, if the breast is given before the mouth knows that it is up to it to respond, this gap is even more evident and more total in the register of meaning. The mother's flow of words is the bearer and creator of meaning, but that meaning only anticipates the infant's capacity to understand it and to act on it. The mother offers herself as a 'speaking I' or an 'I speak' who places the infant in the situation of receiver of discourse, whereas it is beyond his capacity to appropriate the meaning of the statement [...]. (Aulagnier, 2001, p. 10)

If interpretation itself—as a way of naming—becomes persecutory, how would the analytic process actually take place?

I recall a certain moment in Anna's analysis in which she spoke about the need to find a job that would be more profitable than her previous one. Recounting the process of bargaining on her salary she suddenly used extremely low colloquial speech. I listened to her, bewildered, realising that I had never heard her making linguistic mistakes before as she always kept to the strictest grammatical and syntactic rules. Her language was usually so literary that I sometimes wondered whether she understood slang or "street language" at all. When I finally remarked something about it, she said: "Is that what I said? How strange. This is how my mother speaks, and I was always so ashamed of her."

I realise now that through this mistaken, low, colloquial language which came into the session while dealing with issues of separation, Anna enacted between us the very conflict concerning her mother-tongue. It was a delicate moment between us: repeating her exact words would have probably made me deviate from my own way of speaking, or from my own mother-tongue. Speaking "correctly", on the other hand, would have probably sounded like a correction of her speech, or of her mother-tongue, thus taking the risk of shaming her.

Perhaps Anna has unconsciously been trying to tell me something about the narrow, paralysing interval where her emotional language dwelled: her mother-tongue was a broken, hollowed language that dropped truth rather than expressed it. But the literary language Anna adopted suggested no reparation. Instead, it constituted a sort of territorial waters, a zone that posed no danger but was also lifeless, that enabled her to stay alive—but not actually live. A language that excludes "street language" is not a living language. In order to separate and to mourn, in order to speak at all—Anna had to welcome what was formerly thrown out, and contain it within her "body of language" as well as within our relationship.

Plural instead of singular language: reading
The Notebooks of Malte Laurids Brigge *by Rilke*

Malte Laurids Brigge is the last of a line of Danish noblemen that arrives penniless in Paris to become a poet. His writings document the ways in which he tries to turn his reflections, memories, and anxieties into artistic acts and in this way to rehabilitate his life and his personhood. *The Notebooks of Malte Laurids Brigge* is the description of a journey into the unknown, in many respects into that which cannot even be conjectured. It is a journey that gauges the limits of psychic speech up to the point of wondering whether language in itself is a dissociative or a uniting factor.

In the beginning of the book, Malte describes a woman sitting "completely collapsed into herself, forward into her hands", while he walks over to her:

> The woman startled and pulled away too quickly out of herself, too violently, so that her face remained in her two hands. I could see it lying in them, its hollow form. It cost me indescribable effort to stay with those hands and not to look at what had torn itself out of them, I shuddered to see a face from the inside, but still I was much more afraid of the naked flayed head without a face. (Rilke, 1992, p. 16)

What is pseudo-language but that same hollow face-form torn from the inside, a cover disjointed from the exposed, faceless, insufferable interior? Is that interior not exactly what language aims at and evades, acting as a bridge leading us to it, no less than a dividing cover?

Can a non-pseudo-language be created in an analytical work with "hollow face-form" patients? Can the analytical process create a discourse that transforms the insufferable into what can be contained within the inter-subjective field, into an absence that can be carried and shared, and in that respect lend itself to formulation, to denomination?

Above all else, Brigge's journey is a journey to find his poetic language, his private, non-shared language of identity. The chaotic voyage he undergoes in the streets of Paris begins with a distance-less, non-distinct writing, one which takes the qualities of its objects on itself and into itself and ends with the ability to exceed concrete objects and reflect upon them. Malte asks:

> Is it possible that the past is false, because one has always spoken of its masses [...]? Is it possible that one says 'women', 'children', 'boys', not guessing that these words have long since had no plural, but only countless singulars? (Ibid. p. 29)

Malte searches for individual language, for the singular details that have been subsumed and negated into generalities, into the communal, "plural language". What is plural language? An idiom that alienates, privileges sharing over individuality, and therefore fails to distinguish private essences. One could say that pseudo-language is a kind of plural language, or perhaps a language driven by too much of a desire for the shared and the common. It is a language too prone to generalisations, one which makes comparisons but does not differentiate, that evades the private and rejects any exception to the general as well as to the rule. This kind of language—which rejects exceptions—is a language that avoids the process of individuation: a language that does not shift from mother-tongue to individual language or from symbiosis to the differentiated self.

> The third-person is the screen behind which the drama unfolds. He is the noise at the threshold of the voiceless silence of a real conflict. (Ibid. p. 27)

Malte is referring here to the case where the psyche uses the third-person language—not as a means of exceeding and regarding itself, but as a way of exceeding "being itself" or avoiding staying within the experience of the self. In that case, the third-person indeed becomes the partition behind which the drama unfolds, a partition that isolates the liveliness of the first-person experience.

Throughout Malte's Paris journey, he meets time and again those he fears to belong to. He calls them "the outcasts":

> For it is clear to me that these are the outcasts, not simply beggars; […]. They are the refuse, husks of humanity that fate has spewed out. (Ibid. p. 42)

The "outcasts" are those that have no language but that of bodily signs. Those who have no words or do no not use words in order to speak: they allude, they signify, they transmit. They speak a semiotic language that posits no exterior. They are not beggars, since a beggar is someone who lacks something whereas they fundamentally lack their own selves: they "are not" rather than "have not". Perhaps this is why Malte calls them "shells of people"—they are not missing the mantle but rather the content that inhabits it. Malte, too, feels like an outcast: like the outcasts surrounding him he is situated within things rather than outside them:

> It is of this wall I have been speaking all along. One would think I had stood a long time before it; but I'm willing to swear that I began to run as soon as I had recognised that wall. For this is the terrible thing, that I did recognise it. I recognise everything here, and that is why it goes right into me: it is at home in me. (Ibid. p. 48)

Malte's regarding stance is not that of a speaker or that of a listener, but that of a person who has a symbiotic proximity to the things he speaks of. He does not view them from afar—but is assimilated in them. They speak through him. He becomes the smell, the contour or lack thereof; he is close, too close, to everything. He writes out of a dense, speechless sensual experience, despite its wordy excess. This is pseudo-language. Malte is too involved, too imprinted with the things of which he tries to speak. He does not name them—but rather activates them in his own body. "I recognise everything here", he writes, but in fact signifies that identification replaces identity, that same identity which on the one hand allows identification but on the other posits the border that regulates the immediate seeping of things inwards. This line of demarcation is simultaneously the condition of language and that which is established through it.

> Their faces were full of the light that came from the show-booths, and laughter bubbled from their mouths like matter from open

> sores. […] At the crossings people were wedged fast, shoved one
> into the other and there was no forward movement in them, only a
> quiet, gentle swaying back and forth, as if they copulated standing.
> (Ibid. pp. 48–49)

The lack of linear motion also signifies the lack of an inward motion.
Instead of inward motion we receive a kind of endless, roundabout
meandering which is the antithesis of motion in time and space:
a meandering that creates a constant, frozen, spineless present.

Embroiled in horrible distress, Malte imagines himself dying:

> But this time I shall be written. I am the impression that will change.
> (Ibid. p. 52)

The mere fact of his being written—the mere fact of his being
transformed—is experienced as death. It would seem that for those living in the borderless, thick stagnation of the present devoid of living
language—the psychic transformation from experience to word, from
sense to thought—is experienced as a kind of death.

Malte survives like a parasite. He loses himself through contact with
the other, but also keeps himself alive through the other. He cannot bear
it, but can no less separate from it. This parasitical relationship is what
stands at the fundament of language's deconstruction, and at the heart
of its intellectual as against its living use. A parasitical language is a
language that uses the other but does not converse with it: a language
that "swallows" the other and its idiomatic qualities—but does not recognise it as a separate subject, and can therefore have no dialogue with
it. Instead, it becomes that other, simultaneously effacing its otherness
and subsuming it into itself.

What is this parasitical relationship a defence against? Malte describes
a certain unnamed disease, which in effect:

> Drags out of each his deepest danger, that seemed passed, and sets
> it before him again, quite near, imminent. (Ibid, p. 60)

But that recurring danger he is referring to is not the mere re-enactment
of an erroneous action, whatever it may be—but that tangle of insane
memories which hang onto this action "like wet seaweed on some
sunken thing" (ibid, p. 60):

> Lives of which one would never have known mount to the surface
> and mingle with what has actually been, and push aside past
> matters that one had thought to know: for in that which ascends
> is a rested, new strength, but that which has always been there is
> wearied by too frequent remembrance. (Ibid. p. 60)

The nature of the danger, therefore, has nothing to do with the subjects it conjures, but rather with the fact that by a living presentation of
memories forgotten it creates a continuum ("hangs about it like wet seaweed on some sunken thing") which the psyche that refuses to establish
a live language attacks in every possible way. This continuum, which
Malte experiences as a disease, may be just liveliness itself.

"My day, which nothing interrupts, is like a dial without hands", he
writes (ibid. p. 60). When there is no continuum there is nothing that
negates it. It is the exact antithesis of being the owner of a biography.
The mere fact of our having a past makes our present meaningful. As the
form of existence Malte describes contains no history of the self, it lacks
any volume in time and space. Rilke's Malte vacillates between the anxiety that he might disclose all his fears and the anxiety that he won't be
able to say anything since everything is "beyond utterance" (ibid. p. 61).

Why is the "disclosure of a fear" less frightening to him than con-
fronting the "beyond utterance"? The fear that could be exposed is
of a species of fears known to the psyche as such—and in this respect
already inscribed within it. It is a fear already "conversed about"
between him and himself, even if in front of no other, as opposed to
the beyond utterance, which refers to what had never been registered
and therefore never awarded a syntax; to that which was never codified
through language, and is therefore a manifestation of the most primeval, lonely threat.

> My God, if any of it could be shared! But would it *be* then, would
> it *be*? (Ibid. p. 68)

The establishment of a pseudo-language is not just the only way of
preventing contact—but also the only way to preserve it. This point
is fundamental to the understanding of it. Letting things be is in effect
letting ourselves mourn over them and part from them. Their non-
existence within language not only bars us from contact with them

but is paradoxically also the only way of keeping them hidden. The abstinence from establishing a living language is not only an attempt to avoid contact with the absent, but also an attempt to reject the reorganisation of a psyche which had heretofore been consolidated around absence as such.

> Beware of the light that makes space more hollow; [...] Better perhaps to have remained in the darkness, and your unconfined heart would have sought to be the heavy heart of all that is indistinguishable. (Ibid. p. 69)

As opposed to language, which illuminates multiplicity and distinctness—within a symbiosis, where all objects have one "unconfined heart", the conversation between them is neither needed nor possible. Furthermore, the establishment of a language is exactly what could threaten the fantasy of "one heart". This is, as mentioned before, the main function of the pseudo-language: to empty language of its capacity to illuminate distinctness.

Here we arrive at one of the highlights of this collection of writings:

> O stillness in the staircase, stillness from adjoining rooms, stillness high up against the ceiling. O mother: o you only one, who shut out all this stillness, long ago in childhood. Who takes it upon yourself, saying: Don't be afraid, it is I. Who has the courage, all in the night yourself to be this stillness for that which is afraid and perishing with fear. You strike a light, and already the noise is you. [...] You are the light around these familiar intimate things, that are there without afterthought, good, simple, unambiguous. (Ibid. pp. 69–70)

And further:

> But you, you come and hold the monstrous thing behind you, and are in front of it altogether; not like a curtain it can throw open here or there. No, as you had overtaken it at the call that needed you. As if you had come far ahead of anything that may yet happen, and had behind you only your hasting hither, your eternal path, the flight of your love. (Ibid. pp. 69–70)

Even before her willingness to become a language—motherhood is the willingness to be silence. Much before her being the signifier of familiar objects, she is the light around them, that same light that by merely surrounding them makes them unequivocal, innocent, non-threatening objects within the inner world. The mother-tongue is the context within which text can be established, the context within which language can be formed. When the maternal context acts to dilute internal threats then objects become unambiguous and can be named. The steady validity of objects as well as their benevolence is what enables the act of objects' naming and linking. The maternal context is what turns silence into something unthreatening, making it conductive to speech.

The mother, "holding the monstrous thing behind her back", does so through her hasting hither, through her ability to precede "anything that may yet happen". Her ability to supersede the infant's fears and situate herself between the two is what enables him or her to call her name—a name calling that precedes the naming of any object that follows as well.

He further writes:

> Ask no one to speak of you. And when time passes and you find your name getting about among people, take it no more seriously than anything else you find in their mouth. Think rather that it has grown rank, and discard it. Take another, any other, so that god may call you in the night. And conceal it from everyone. (Ibid. p. 74)

What's in a name? A name is the first gift given to us by an-other. But a name is also the first symbol of otherness since the only need to use the naming faculty at all is the existence of an-other. Can that other name us without us experiencing the very act of naming as a sacrilege of the most private name, the name by which God can "call us in the night"?

When the mother who gives her child a name is also experienced as desecrating the name's privacy, then the urge to establish a language of names is transformed into an urge to reject naming at all, hence to abstain from speech. In those circumstances speech itself is experienced not as expressing one's most private essence but as robbing him or her of it.

> Then you set about that unexampled act of violence in your work, which ever more impatiently, ever more desperately, sought equivalents among the visible for the inwardly seen. (Ibid. p. 76)

The very act of naming proceeds to tear off "the face" from the interior, like the image described at the very beginning of this book, leaving it exposed, defenceless, and meaningless.

"It is as if they had destroyed beforehand the words with which one might grasp them", Malte writes of women (ibid. p. 120). It may be argued, though, that he is not writing about all women, but of the one mother. That primeval, mythological mother internalised beyond any words, which no word can reach. Not only the mother who wills to be the silence—but the one whose most exact representation would be silence, since she is the beyond utterance itself. That mother whose proximity (and loss) all language is fundamentally established to achieve; to apprehend her only to discover that she is not susceptible to apprehension but through the wordless body, the body that precedes words.

> Sometimes I reflect on how heaven came to be and death: through our having distanced what is most precious to us […]. (Ibid. p. 145)

As if the very act of creation, from birth to death, comes from our having distanced something dear and having filled the space left behind with thoughts and words. The absence of affinity to objects outside stirs death anxieties. But in order to "think" that anxiety one must create and tolerate that absence. Alternatively, if it is the affinity to the object rather than the object itself that we distance ourselves from—then no language will be created, as it will be impossible to create a distance that would allow the missing object to be reborn in thought.

Speaking of the lover, Malte says:

> Her devotion wants to be immeasurable; that is her happiness. But the nameless suffering of her love has always been this: that she is required to restrict this devotion. (Ibid. p. 176)

The very shift from the idea of love to love itself, perhaps like the mother's shift from the idea of motherhood to her actual motherhood, is in itself an act of working through loss, perhaps like the mourning of language, which seeks to encompass everything but finds itself reduced to that which can be apprehended. The mother's shift from the idea of the child to the actual child is what allows that child to establish language. The very possibility of establishing language hinges upon the depressive accomplishment of this imperceptible, sometimes insufferable, shift from the idea to the thing-in-itself.

Epilogue

Rilke's controversial piece ends with an essay on the prodigal son returning home at the end of his journey:

> It was possible to be the whole army or a commander on horseback or a ship on the ocean, according to the way one felt. [...] but however numerous the imaginings that came to one, in between there was always time to be nothing but a bird. (Ibid. p. 211)

What is "being a bird" about? It is perhaps the freedom of language at its best. Not just the freedom to move effortlessly between thousands of different face-masks—always knowing that one's face is waiting there, underneath, ready to shine through—but also to be, at least at times, free of a story or a storytelling language, just like that bird whose crossing the air demarcates the limits of space.

Malte returns home and at once becomes—

> The person for whom, out of his little past and their own wishes, they had long fashioned a life; the creature belonging to them all, who stood day and night under the suggestion of their love, between their hope and their suspicion, before their blame or praise. (Ibid. p. 211)

The great threat of communal language is that it does not only contradict the individual's, but actually annihilates the non-communal, evaporates the liberty of being something un-haunted by any attempt to name and comprehend. The return of the prodigal son does not efface the horse, or the leader riding it, or the boat on the high seas. It effaces the bird. It annihilates that unconverted freedom that cannot be transformed, that conditions the will to share and hence the will to establish any language at all; that freedom, shared by those for whom language it is not only roots but wings—not only to be the owner of "a different story", but to be, at least for a moment, story-less.

How to create a language whose words do not become a filter through which truth is actually being dropped? Perhaps by a willingness to meet our most private street language, the one that holds the contents that were thrown out, the contents from which we were expropriated by our own selves. Perhaps by understanding that even the most precise articulation involves not only what is imprecise but also what is unsayable: that which becomes—through the very inability to express it—the abyss that lies beneath all words as well as their deepest resonance.

CHAPTER TWO

The split between voice and meaning: the dual function of psychotic syntax*

Psychotic development and potentiality

One of the most obscure and interpretatively appealing issues within the field of psychoanalytic thinking is the issue of psychotic development.

Grotstein (1990), when dealing with the psychotic experience of the "black hole", claims that a general clinical conclusion one can infer from neurobiological research is that neurobiological deficits seem to impart specific defects or generalised deficits; manifestations of this latter category being an overall sense of hypersensitivity to experience or irritability, a sort of "mental allergy" to frustration. This imposes of course a greater challenge to motherhood—made even more complex when the mother herself suffers from the same hereditary disorder. Hartmann (1939, 1953), in differentiating between apparatuses of primary and secondary autonomy, listed that of a "threshold" as one of the former, and implicated it in schizophrenia. Freud (1920g) had already postulated

---

*This chapter is based on the paper: Amir, D. (2010). The split between voice and meaning: The dual function of psychotic syntax. *International Forum of Psychoanalysis*, 19(1): 34–42. Reprinted by permission of Taylor & Francis (http://www.tandfonline.com).

the importance of the stimulus barrier as being of critical importance in the phenomenon of psychic trauma. But it was Benjamin (1965) who distinguished between passive and active stimulus barriers, declaring the former to be an initial, temporary biological default and the latter to be the activity of the protective environment, a distinction hinted at by Hartmann (1953) as well. Grotstein goes on and claims that all these contributors viewed the stimulus barrier or threshold from the standpoint of ego psychology. It was Bion (1962b), by redefining secondary process as "alpha function", who clarified another side of this concept. Bion hypothesised that the psychotic suffers from an inability to transform his or her experiences into mental elements via alpha function and therefore becomes "bombarded" by random, no-longer-meaningful "beta elements" that cluster around him as "nameless dread".

In the course of his work with psychotic patients Bion learned that the psychotic person—or the psychotic component in everyone's personality—is unable to suffer the psychological reality. This is why the psychotic individual resists any shift in the direction of cognitive formation. Under normal conditions, the individual holds experiences in his mind for long enough to allow alpha function to become operative and mitigate them. Hence, the process of thinking provides a degree of containment for painful experiences and makes them more tolerable. The psychotic person, in contrast, is unable to suffer frustration or moderate it by means of thought. Thus he must continue managing the psychological stress by evacuating it through the muscular system. What is discharged is the unthinkable emotional experience, or, in other words, beta elements which cannot pass through the psyche's alpha function. This is how the psychotic person evacuates his psyche while staying trapped within his structure of consciousness, without the escape route offered by thinking. In this way, his mind finds itself in a state of gradual starvation. Threatened by the persecutory feelings that accompany it, the psychotic person tries to annihilate all consciousness of his psychic reality. Any process of integration arouses great resistance in him because it may put the broken fragments back together into one entity, and this will force the psychotic person to deal with a cruel and terrorising super-ego. Bion, thus, observed a mental process that fails to occur in the psychotic part of the personality and whose absence or destruction cause psychotic patients to manifest a severe deficiency in everything involving the mental ability to pay attention, to remember, to judge, and to generate visual-associative images. He understood that the psychotic patient actively attacks this function in order to avoid integration. In so doing, he therefore bars himself from the input necessary for psychological development (Bion, 1962a, 1962b).

The psychotic, for whom dealing with reality involves unbearable pain, "rejects" beta elements by turning them into bizarre objects rather than allowing them to be processed by alpha function, therefore failing to turn the primary into the secondary. This refusal to accept reality stems from the encounter with unnamable elements whose acidity consumes the psychic digestive system. The psychotic's only defence against them is by establishing psychotic zones within normal thinking (that is, areas of non-thinking), or developing a general psychosis.

What are these elements whose acidity prevents digestion?

Grotstein (1990b) claims that the schizophrenic suffers from a deficit in primary narcissism. This can be conceived of as the absence or compromise in the experience of bonding (by mother or father) and attachment by the infant. The infant may be stressed in attachment by an inborn deficit in being able to receive nurture and to offer an intersubjectively cooperative form of behaviour toward the mother so as to participate in an interdependent experience. Furthermore, the mother's body, mind, and soul, particularly as organised by her intuition, reverie and preoccupation, serve as primal regulators of her infant's physical and mental states. Thus bonding, attachment, holding, and containment serve compositely as basic "selfobject" functions so as to create a background of safety (Sandler, 1960), a holding environment (Winnicott, 1960b), the development of the container and the contained (Bion, 1962b), a rhythm of safety (Tustin, 1988), a background selfobject (or presence) of primary identification (Grotstein, 1980), and the development of the matrix (Ogden, 1986); all of which constitute different ways of conceiving primary narcissism. Grotstein proffers the image of Siamese twins to reconcile the developmental paradox in which the infant can be conceived of as separate and not separate at the same time (dual track). The future schizophrenic may conceivably suffer from a deficit in primary narcissism, or from the impingements and neglectfulness of the environment, which may be so critical that pathological secondary narcissism develops that may negate an already formed primary narcissism retrospectively. Grotstein employs the term "black hole" to designate the fundamental experience of being psychotic. He claims that the black hole phenomenon, as described by psychotic and borderline patients, generally designates a hapless or precipitous fall into endless space. The term, according to him, is commonly used by a large number of patients who suffer from primitive emotional disturbances and designates the experience of floorlessness, boundarilessness, a sense of extreme precariousness, and of imminent disaster. Grotstein claims that there seems to be a difference between the sense of emptiness or hollowness that depressed patients and some borderlines describe— and the experience of the black hole described by these others. What they have in common, however, is the sense of meaninglessness.

Piera Aulagnier (2001) addresses in her writings several factors that may foretell psychotic potentiality. The first is the absence of the father from the discourse of the "word-bearer" (the mother), an absence that leaves the infant exposed to the incestuous contents that the mother was unable to repress and from which the very presence of the father did not shield the child.[1] The second factor is the mother's failure to repress her incestuous wish directed at her own mother. What the mother desires is indeed not the birth of a new subject, but rather her own rebirth by her mother. Her wish for rebirth is in effect a death wish directed at her newborn, for what she desires is not its birth as an owner of its future but rather as an object through which she may reconstitute her own past. The third factor is related to the identificatory void caused by the mother's inability to provide historical and emotional context for the preverbal experiences inscribed in the infant's body, experiences which the infant is unable to remember. The lack of maternal discourse— which would gather these experiences into a narrative form, just as it would bring together various body parts to form a holistic, pleasurable experience of the body—does not allow the infant to have the essential physical and psychic experience necessary for the emergence of the self. The fourth factor is the mother's refusal to allow the infant its separate existence and its own thoughts. Her need to understand and to articulate every psychic zone denies the infant's right to privacy and autonomous thinking, turning it into a sort of satellite-object utterly subjected to her authority. In effect, the mother's control over the infant's thoughts is a denial of her death wish toward it: not thinking the thoughts she forbids it to think, it will not know what she forbids it to know. Her denied death wish toward her child is expressed in her behaviour—yet unknown to her, just as she utterly denies her incestuous wish toward her mother. In other words, the mechanism of repression which is typical of neurotic development is replaced by the mechanism of denial which is typical of psychotic development. While the mother has not repressed that which must be repressed—what has not been repressed must not be exposed to either the infant or herself. In order to avoid the danger involved in any exposure of that unconscious desire for the death (or un-birth) of her child, the mother forbids it any contact with whatever may be associated with that desire. The fear of breaching the prohibition imposed upon knowing invokes a sense of catastrophe in the child whenever it draws close to an understanding. The prohibition to understand may turn into a prohibition to assimilate any experience into memory, thus creating "holes in memory" where entire parts of the subject's history are erased, eliminating all significance from potentially catastrophic situations.

In his article "Shadows, ghosts and chimaeras: on some early modes of handling psycho-genetic heritage", Joshua Durban quotes a well-known Zen riddle (a Koan) that asks: "What was the shape of your face before you were born?" (Durban, 2011). This is indeed the pivotal question: what was the representation of the infant in its mother's mind prior to its birth? Was that infant an echo of her death wish or of her life wish?

As we have seen, psychotic potentiality is indeed connected, according to Aulagnier, to the nature and significance of the child's representation in his mother's mind prior to its birth, when it was still nothing but a "spoken shadow". In fact, she sees psychosis as a development of a self that was unable to find answers to questions pertaining to its origins. In the absence of a "maternal discourse" that would provide the subject with a history, the infant is confronted with an unbearable void, which it fills with "primary delusional structure"—a structure that replaces the normal causal logic which according to Aulagnier specifies the discourse of others which abides by common rules of speech and thought. In other words, the child deals with the emptiness of lacking a continuous experience of self by constructing an experience of delusional continuity, but since that continuity is completely idiosyncratic it isolates the subject rather than makes it part of the common discourse.

From the perspective of the potential psychotic, all autonomous thought or feeling is prohibited. Unable to construct a context of logical causality that would allow a continuous perception of the self (and would allow the subject to see itself as continuous)—it cannot but construct meaning which is incompatible with the discourse of others. In order to turn the unutterable and the meaningless into something meaningful, the subject creates a delusional causal structure. This could be seen as a means of restoring a previously prohibited autonomy, at the price of its turning into an underground one, far away both from the mother's and the public's eyes. Once prohibited the construction of an autonomous syntax, the subject creates a "non-syntactic" syntax by means of which an illusion of continuity is generated. In this sense, the schizophrenic's delusion may be seen as an expression of his or her struggle for the right to exist.

From the moment it is born, the psychotic's self has to defend itself against the death wish directed at it. That death wish, according to Aulagnier, originates in the mother's desire to return to the pleasure of her own birth, thus fulfilling her own mother's desire. In this respect, the newborn is the fruit of the mother's incestuous relationship with her own mother. It is not born out of the pleasure and the desire of a couple; the father, as a third that may separate the two women (mother and daughter), is totally annihilated. The mother cannot actually foresee any "future self" of her child since it only exists in her fantasy as a means of returning to her own past. Thus "the schizophrenic has not, nor will he ever have, any access to the order of temporality." (Aulagnier, 2001).

By heading towards the past instead of towards the future, the common, objective, cosmic order is reversed. As if the child is born backwards, in order to reconstruct something rather than create something new. Being given to the mother's mother—who doesn't want it either but only uses it to repeat the pleasure of her daughter's birth—it has no place in the mother's psychic space, nor can it create a psychic space of its own. It would seem that the basic element missing from the psychotic's development, according to Aulagnier, is the mother's ability to confer on the infant its own distinct meaning. She imparts her own meaning to it—or else gives it no meaning at all. The child thus exists as an object rather than as a subject. In view of that the attack on the entire process of producing language can be understood. The psychotic language is not a language in its own right but rather a shelter that sustains an illusion of being in dialogue with the outside and the other, while in fact it is an autarkical economy that neither communicates with the outside nor takes it into consideration. This pattern is of course a repetition of the mother's mindset towards her infant: her language does not function as a platform on the basis of which the child will in due course establish its own language. She does not reach out to the infant nor does she take it into consideration, but rather she appropriates it to serve her own psychic economy. Aulagnier refers to the lack of a unified experience of the body, an experience imparted to the child by the mother's voice naming each and every body organ. The voice signifies the mother's presence, while silence signifies a desire for annihilation. The fact that hearing cannot seal itself off (the child cannot "shut" its ears), Aulagnier claims, accentuates the persecutory character of the voice typical of psychosis. The psychotic has no escape from the tormenting voice, neither by understanding the uttered content (since understanding is prohibited) nor by hushing the voice itself.

Following both Bion's and Aulagnier's ideas, this chapter seeks to examine two functions of the development of psychotic syntax within the non-psychotic personality. The first function is that of producing a split between voice and meaning in the mother–infant relationship, a split whose aim is to disengage contact with contents that cannot be metabolized, associated with the mother's denied death wish toward her infant. The second function pertains to the use of psychotic syntax as a way of denying separateness and annihilating the "speaking I". In conclusion, psychotic language will be discussed as a "hybrid language" generated by an incestuous relationship between the mother-tongue and the infant's.

The experience of not being able to understand, often accompanying therapeutic and analytic work with patients who have a psychotic syntax, is one of the burdens that hinder their containment. The following discussion is not referring to psychotic patients, but rather to patients whose personality organisation is not defined as psychotic and yet develops a "semi-psychotic" language that impedes both communication and understanding. This is in effect an enactment, within the transference relationship, of the infant's chaotic experience within the mother–infant linguistic unit. If persecutory rules are imposed upon the primary linguistic unit, and its hub is not love but the prohibition against love, then speech turns from an act that expresses unavoidable "primary violence" (Aulagnier, 2001) to one expressing "secondary violence" (that is, violence in its ordinary form), and the attack on the regular syntax becomes the only way by which the pain it inflicts may be prevented or moderated.

The defence of the psychotic child against the mother occurs by way of an attack on the presence of voice and the presence of meaning, and even more so by an attack on the unity of voice and meaning—a monstrous union representing the link to primary unrepressed prohibitions. Such an attack creates blind spots within language related to contents that have not been repressed by the mother—and that the infant is not permitted to see, to think, or to remember.

The linguistic split that the infant creates is its only way of establishing a zone that is exterior to the territory of prohibited thoughts and to the scope of maternal control which might unveil them. Through the experience of non-meaning and the ongoing attack on causality, the infant defends itself against an all-seeing, all-knowing mother. By creating a delusional linguistic structure it provides itself with a language of its own, an alternative continuity that the mother cannot follow. Thus the psychotic syntax not only creates a split between voice and meaning, but also between self and other.

The developmental urge to speak, to understand, to link, is replaced by the urge to destroy meaning, to disconnect, not to know. In many of these cases an indifferent, affectless tone of voice is used in an attempt to avoid any exposure to emotion. Speech itself thus enacts the split between content and tone, as the apathetic, monotonous tone of voice repeats the attack on the subject's presence (to which his or her voice testifies), while the fragmented contents or the "non-syntax" repeats the attack on the ability to create meaning. Psychotic syntax has a dual function: it protects one from madness by means of madness. It creates continuity where alternative syntax rules apply—or rather rules of non-syntax—aiming to rid the mother–infant unit of both separateness and grief. Psychosis thus not only expresses the "unspeakable"—but is also a way of speaking that which must not be spoken or known. It encrypts what must not be known into a secret code, concealed even from the speaker him or herself. The psyche consigns to that psychotic code whatever it cannot consign to consciousness. The split it creates between voice and meaning becomes a split between a concealing and a revealing consciousness, between the need to decode and the need to encode. The maternal split presence, giving life to the infant on the one hand and driven by a death wish on the other, conveys to the infant a dual message that does not allow it to focus. Oscillating incessantly between the dimension of voice and the dimension of meaning, the infant is never able to combine them into a unified three-dimensional experience.

The zones of such a split which are present in the language and syntax of non-psychotics always attest to something unspeakable, unknowable, that must be encoded so that it may be spoken without being understood—or understood without having to be spoken.

The physical inability to shut one's ears is significant because it symbolises the existence of messages or contents that the infantile psyche is unable to regulate or defend itself against. Faced with such messages, the psyche employs other means of regulation or avoidance. While ears cannot be shut down, a voice may however be fragmented into meaningless auditory units and its contents may be encoded into a language that does not constitute continuity or sense, thus avoiding digestion. The psychotic zones within language indeed indicate that the psyche is struggling against a tone that must be neutralised or against a content that must be disintegrated. One may assume that the infant's first disintegrating encounter was with maternal voice and contents. One may also assume that the mother herself employed the very same disintegrating mechanism against the intensity of the infant's presence, or against the intensity of the maternal experience, or against the intensity of the maternal object's persecuting presence within her. The infant thus develops a psychotic language both as an internalisation of the mother and as a defence against her.

Clinical illustration I

Benjamin, in his early twenties, is referred to therapy by his psychiatrist with a diagnoses of major depression accompanied with utter social isolation. Despite being a handsome young man, his facial expression is sealed and his gestures are bizarre. He inserts fingers into his mouth as he speaks as if trying to push the words back in instead of uttering them out loud. The few sentences he utters usually end with the words "I don't know." This is not a coincidental combination of words. Benjamin refuses to know and no less refuses to become attached. He is not schizophrenic, but his interpersonal discourse does not follow normative emotional and linguistic rules. He usually speaks in broken sentences, mumbling, as if speaking to himself rather than to his interlocutor, looking at the ceiling or floor, and rolling his eyes. It appears that his understanding of the other's discourse, too, doesn't correspond with the latter's intentions; what he hears is usually different from what was said, mostly with a paranoid shade indicating a somewhat faulty reality testing. His tone of voice is dull and monotonous, showing no affect, lacking any signs of punctuation.

His appearance is as strange as his speech. He wears short-sleeved shirts even on the coldest of winter days, mostly inside-out. When I ask about that he replies, as usual, that he doesn't know why, but that's how it has always been. I understand that wearing a shirt inside-out is similar to his pushing words in rather than out, or to the way he constructs a non-language, or non-syntax, rather than one that makes sense. He is extremely unkempt and dirty, neglects his body and does not treat any physical problem, not even when he is in pain. One day, arriving with his face swollen, he tells me that his teeth ache. When I ask him why he doesn't have them treated he replies, to my surprise, that he can't stand for anyone to push fingers into his mouth. I suddenly realise that psychotherapy, too, is a way of shoving fingers into his mouth, into his cavities of speech or deeper yet, wondering whether the reason he speaks with his fingers deep in his mouth is also connected to his unwillingness to allow me to insert my own fingers (or words) there.

Benjamin describes his mother as a hard, persecutory and intrusive woman who had not only despised him since his early years for his strangeness and peculiarity but also never listened to his signs of distress. Even when he begged her to allow him to be discharged from compulsive military service on psychiatric grounds, feeling that he couldn't stand to stay there for one more day, even when he threatened to commit suicide, she still pressured him to stay. Having lost her own brother in the war, she could have had him discharged by merely signing a form but refused to do so, claiming that he must deal with it without any concessions. His father is perceived as weak, dependent, almost voiceless besides the mother's high, shrill voice—which Benjamin claims he cannot bear to hear. Speaking to her on the telephone, he feels like flinging the phone down to escape the awful vibrations that her voice conveys to him. Often he can't even recall what she said to him, being so preoccupied with the attempt not to hear her voice. When I ask what is so troubling about her voice he mumbles, looking at his shoe tips: "It's like inserting a bug into your ear. It hurts your ear. You can't bear it. You simply can't." "You?" I repeat. "You," he says, "that is ... me."

This was possibly the first time since his therapy began that he looked straight at me. And it was possibly the first time I felt that I understood something about him. I understood that vis-à-vis his mother it was prohibited to be an "I". I understood that his way of surviving her intrusiveness was to disown himself to the point that he no longer existed in the first-person, or as an "I", perhaps because the first-person, the "I", was the one that contained pain. The fact that the first-person became the second-person in moments of expressing truths was related to never having been allowed to exist in the first-person—that is, as a speaking subject, as a subject that had a voice.

One day, Benjamin arrived to our appointment a few minutes early, and while standing in the lane by my house my dog barked at him. Being in the garden, behind a fence, it posed no danger to Benjamin. Nevertheless when he entered the room he was more upset than I'd ever seen him before, stuttering that he hated dogs, mumbling broken sentences, fingers deep in his mouth, about a student who once set fire to his neighbour's dog because its barking had disturbed his studies for a mid-term test.

I understood that he was telling me something about the intensity of his hatred and rage, about his jealousy of someone I love, perhaps even warning me against his homicidal wish towards whoever takes his place or threatens it. At the same time, I sensed he was also telling me something about the meaning of noise for him. The dog's barking, piercing his ears without his being able to defend against it, provoked the same helpless rage that his mother's voice used to provoke. His homicidal wish towards it was his wish towards his mother as well as towards me for not stopping the barking and preventing the voice's intrusiveness. The intrusion of voice was even more difficult for him than the intrusion of meaning, and also preceded it. He used to disassemble meaning by diverting the thought, by fragmenting sentences, by his erasing of my questions each time anew with the "I don't know" by which he ended every utterance. The voice, however, was much more difficult to nullify. It penetrated under his skin, set him off and made him lose control. Long before he could understand what his mother was saying to him, her voice was an insupportable, unbearable stimulus. It was that unbearable stimulus against which he set up a psychotic language, the only defence he could afford against that very intrusion: as a psychotic, he left her unable to understand him, thus defending himself against her understanding—which, like her voice, was a violent, intolerable intrusion. The psychotic language produced a safe haven in which, while not sheltered from her voice, he was beyond the reach of her insights. His finger-shoving into his mouth indicated that the gesture of disarming the voice was also displaced to his own voice and words and was also being enacted within the therapeutic relations with me. Not only was it hard to hear his voice, it was also extremely difficult to understand the words he uttered. In other words, since he couldn't shut his ears against my words, he shut his own mouth, preventing me from understanding his words. If I couldn't understand him, I couldn't intrude on him. Rilke writes in the first of his *Duino Elegies*:

> Who, if I cried, would hear me, of the angelic orders?
> Or even supposing that one should suddenly
> Carry me to his heart—I should perish under the pressure
> Of his stronger nature. (Rilke, 2000)

In a sense, this is the most accurate formulation of the state through which a psychotic syntax is established: the greatest wish is to be the one whose cry is heard among "angelic orders". However, the recipient of that cry crushes it as it carries it to its heart. It is a choice between being unheard (by not being understood) and perishing under the pressure of the other's intensive nature of understanding. Psychotic syntax may be seen as a cry that is heard but not understood, thereby producing or setting in motion a defensive situation in which the other would hear the speaker without crushing it—since his inability to provide that voice with meaning would prevent it from carrying it to his heart.

Clinical illustration II

Karin, an art student in her early thirties, seeks therapy due to difficulties in forming close relationships as well as acute anxieties about any possible sexual intercourse. As the daughter of a schizophrenic mother whose illness broke out in Karin's childhood—and to whose psychotic episodes she was closely exposed—she has developed a language with psychotic characteristics. Her tone of voice, much like Benjamin's, is monotonous, lacking musical dynamics, its rhythm constant and unchanging. Her syntax is extremely disjointed, missing crucial conjunctions. It is often impossible to know where one sentence ends and another begins, each swallowed by the next, as if chronically opening up parentheses within parentheses, only partially closing them or neglecting to do so altogether. The contents of her speech tend to become mixed in a very similar way, drifting from one subject to another, creating long, pointless monologues characterised by sheer associative looseness, often lacking a "narrator's intent" or a "narrator position."

From her fragmented life story I understand that Karin, who throughout her childhood used to take care of her mother during her psychotic episodes—bathing, feeding, and cleaning her up like a baby—has developed a language that denied separation, a language within which the mother felt less anomalous and Karin herself felt less lonely. The discourse she has developed with me was very similar in nature to her symbiotic (and semiotic) discourse with her mother, which merged their languages together to a degree that Karin's narrating "I" completely disappeared from it. That joint psychotic discourse seemed to sustain the illusion that they were indistinct from each other, an illusion that preserved yet another illusion—the illusion that the mother was not ill. At the same time, the lack of separation between them also sustained the illusion that Karin herself was not ill. Karin's unconscious fantasy was that should the languages be separated it may be discovered that not only was the mother insane, but she, too, carried that insanity within her. Maintaining her psychotic discourse with her mother paradoxically alleviated her fear of being left alone with that illness. As the entire psychotic discourse was founded on the denial of separation, it also denied grief, concession, rage and horror. There was something omnipotent, all consuming about this discourse, yet also very vulnerable and fragile.

I retrospectively realised that it was Karin's father who had assigned her the mission of curing the mother of her madness, since in his fantasy—and probably the mother's, too—it was Karin's birth that had brought on that madness in the first place. In Aulagnier's terms it might be said that it was the experience of motherhood that produced the death wish towards the little child (and it was in order to prevent the acknowledgment of that death wish that the act of fragmentation became so necessary), probably reviving also the grandmother's (the mother's mother) death wish towards the mother herself. Unable to cure her mother, Karin took on her illness. In order not to know what mustn't be known, and at the same time avoiding a contact with the mother's madness, Karin developed a "circumventing" language within which the mother's speech became meaningful. In that way she succeeded in generating an experience of context, of historicity, of continuity and identity yet without exposing her mother's death wish toward her, a death wish which was manifested throughout her childhood in severely neglectful and violent behaviours. The father's distance, completely waiving away his vital presence as a representative of the "discourse of others" or as a buffer between his wife and his daughter, left Karin locked within that private psychotic discourse with no choice but applying its rules to her contacts with the rest of the world too.

It is for good reason that Karin sought therapy for anxiety related to sexual relationships. In order to realise herself sexually as a woman, she needed not only to separate from her mother but also, perhaps above all, risk becoming a mother herself, that is to say—becoming homicidal and insane like her own mother.

Psychotic language as a hybrid language

Psychotic hybrid language (that is, zones of psychotic syntax in a non-psychotic personality) is generated when rather than serving as a platform on which the infant's language may develop—the mother's language imposes itself on the infant's language, violating thereby its intimacy by enforcing hers. The centre of gravity within the mother–infant unit is thus shifted: it does not relate to the baby but rather stems from the mother's own need to be contained. In effect, there is an incestuous relationship between the mother's language and the infant's, in which the mother forces her own syntactic rules on her infant, while it, being immature enough to digest them, ingests or assimilates these rules with neither digestion nor filtering involved. The infant's speech, thus, enacts its mother's domineering rules instead of using them to create its own living language. The intimate attack on the infant, launched by the mother's needs, creates a new linguistic entity. This linguistic entity is neither the mother's language nor the infant's, but rather a hybrid one that gives expression to non of them, aiming instead to preserve their un-separateness. The hub of it is not a fertile dialogue between languages but rather one language malignantly imposing itself on another. That forced intercourse is the opposite of dialogue, the opposite of conversation, the opposite of a relationship. This hybrid language has no more similarity to a living language than an incestuous relationship would have to a sexual relationship between loving adults.

The hybrid language's adult manifestations will find expression in the generalisation of that inadequate syntax to all linguistic zones. While the personality does not conform with a psychotic diagnosis, the language and its use will be characterised by associative looseness, vagueness, fragmentation, a sort of "anti-syntax" and an utter lack of narrator's position or a "speaking I". Rather than an infantile-subject's language generated from an adult subject's language, a hybrid language is generated which contains many adult characteristics (such as sophisticated words) alongside an infantile syntax that annihilates meaning—all in the context of an indifferent, monotonous tone of voice, which in itself constitutes an attack on meaning as well as on the other's attentiveness. The overall structure of this language serves as a denial of separateness, and is thus an attack on the infantile psychic birth. Once the infantile self is revealed, so is the death wish directed at it, putting its life at risk. Therefore, the infant's only way of avoiding risk is to avoid being born in the first-person or as an autonomous self. Enacting this pattern within any relationship generates a dialogue in which the other, not recognising the speaker as a separate entity, would not direct a death wish toward it. Thus this linguistic hybrid serves at the same time both as a denial of the other's separateness and as a concealment of the self from the other. In this sense, it may be seen as an attack on language rather than as a language in its own right.

Paul Celan's beautiful poem "Speak you too" (Celan, 1995, pp. 79–81[2]) is probably one of the most powerful illustrations of the function of this hybrid language:

> Speak you too,
> Speak as the last,
> Say out your say.
>
> Speak—
> But don't split off No from Yes.
> Give your say this meaning too:
> Give it the shadow.
> Give it shadow enough,
> Give it as much
> As you know it spread round you from
> Midnight to midday and midnight.
>
> Look around:
> See how things all come alive—
> By death! Alive!
> Speaks true who speaks shadow.

But now the place shrinks, where you stand:
Where now, shadow-stripped, where?
Climb. Grope upwards.
Thinner you grow, less knowable, finer!
Finer: a thread
The star wants to descend on:
So as to swim down bellow, down here
Where it sees itself shimmer: in the swell
Of wandering words.

The command "Speak you too, Speak as the last, Say out your say" implies that someone else speaks for the speaker. "See how things all come alive—By death": through the shadow of death, the speaker comes to life. It is the (m)other's death wish that begets the infant, and the infant realises and enacts it by turning from an infant into the other's shadow. "Speaks true who speaks shadow": the only truthful speech is that which does not deny the shadow of the death wish. But that is precisely what the speaker is prohibited to know or to say. Now, having clung to truth ("Speaks true who speaks shadow"), the speaker's place gradually shrinks ("Where now, shadow-stripped, where?"). The child that has exposed the shadow of the (m)other's death wish toward it has no place and no way to exist. It must grope its way upwards as it evaporates, getting thinner and thinner, until it turns from a living speaker into a thread that connects heaven and earth: that which seeks to be born ("to swim down bellow, down here") and realised on earth—and the "swell of wandering words" that never assemble into an integrated, integrating language; that never stabilise into a "discourse of others", a biography, an identity, but rather remains an occasional flicker that never accumulates weight or volume. The wandering sands metaphor is most apt for the hybrid language described here. The infantile self flickers through it, but never lingers long enough to be accumulated in terms of historicity, of causality, of context. Once the (m)other's death wish toward the child is exposed and stripped bare, facing the infantile self—the infant has no place by that (m)other's side. It must then adopt a psychotic language that denies the death wish by denying separateness. As long as the infantile self is not fully distinct from the maternal self, the latter will harbour no death wish toward it. Thus the infant turns itself into a shadow—not just the shadow of the (m)other's death wish, but a shadow of its own existence. It flickers through the wandering sands, at times as an enactment of the death wish and at times as an enactment of the wish for life. Yet the "yes and no" (the "yes" of the wish for life and the "no" of the death wish) cannot be united, for such an unity ("don't split off No from Yes") might bring the infantile self to confront contents that it cannot bear.

The two possible escape routes from such an exposure of the (m)other's death wish towards the infantile self are either avoiding language or avoiding existence itself. That is, one must prevent the very creation of language so that an autonomously thinking self would not emerge, and to prevent the creation of a thinking self so that the death wish towards it would not be exposed. The psychotic language adopted by the infantile self ultimately serves both: it prevents an exposure of the (m)other's death wish—by thwarting the development of an autonomous infantile self who may activate that death wish. The infantile self actually saves itself by becoming a shadow, flickering through the words "wandering sands" without endowing them with meaning, without ever being able to become a body that has a shadow of its own.

CHAPTER THREE

The chameleon language of perversion*

In her paper "Perversion is us?" Muriel Dimen writes:

> Perversion, even in Freud's understanding, let alone in light of the cultural revolution that has taken place since the 1960s, challenges our intellect, our passion, our practice. (Dimen, 2001)

What is perversion?

Freud (1905d, 1919e, 1922b, 1923e, 1927e, 1930a, 1940e) thought of perverse sexuality as an arrested state of infantile sexuality in adults who feared an experience of castration awaiting them on the threshold of the oedipal phase. Perversion constitutes the breach of a social barrier, that of the "law of the father" (Lacan, 1958), which channels sexuality for the purpose of procreation. By transgressing this law, the perverse subject becomes situated in the field of infantile sexuality and fixation which negates the prohibition against incest along with the fact of castration.

---

*This chapter is based on the paper: Amir, D. (2013). The chameleon language of perversion. *Psychoanalytic Dialogues*, 23: 393–407. Reprinted by permission of Taylor & Francis (http://www.tandfonline.com).

Thus, the perverse subject's mother is perceived as omnipotent, in possession of penis as well as breasts, an object that lacks nothing.

Conceptualisations of perversion have deepened with time, as analytic thinkers moved from conceiving of it as a defence against oedipal castration anxiety to thinking of perverse relations as serving to protect a crumbling, possibly pre-psychotic self (Stein, 2005). Glover (1933) regarded perversion as a function that contained and isolated the psychotic parts of the personality, allowing other parts to proceed normally. Glasser (1986), in his discussion of perversity, gave a central place to the core complex which emerges in the early childhood of the perverse subject as the result of a yearning for absolute fusion with the object together with the terror of annihilation that comes with an invasive maternal presence. The perverse solution generates intense relations with the object but takes a sadomasochistic control of the annihilating intimate fusion. Stoller (1974, 1975, 1991) argued that perversity is the erotic form of hatred. He made a distinction between perversion, which originates in hostility, and varieties of sexuality that do not originate in hostility. The perverse act, he argued, conceals fantasies of revenge and hurts the loved object, thus transforming childhood trauma into adult triumph. Joseph (1971) explained perverse sexual arousal in the analytic session as an attack on both the patient's and the analyst's ability to think, something that happens through the continuous sexualisation of the transference and of the act of thinking itself.

In a chapter entitled "The perverse subject of analysis", Ogden (1999) suggests that perversion results from a core experience of psychic death. The perverse subject is a baby still-born as a result of his parents' empty and lifeless relationship. Perversion is the compulsive erotisation of that void in order to trigger excitement which is unconsciously experienced as a false substitute. Ogden focuses attention on the empty analytical relationship, that is, the empty analytical discourse, and the way a perverse intersubjective analytic "Third" emerges in the course of the analysis. This "perverse subject of analysis" actually constitutes the empty erotic drama that develops on the analytic stage. The aim of this drama, a co-production of analyst and patient, is to forge the illusion that the subject is an actually living subject—in order to avoid the experience of psychological death and the recognition of the death of the analytic encounter. As McDougall (1982) also claimed, the perverse patient actually mobilises the other for a recurrent enactment of the fantasy of entering the parents' primal scene, a fantasy which is life threatening. Simultaneously, the perverse subject has a deluded sense that he can approach the fire without getting burned. The perverse subject feels immune to danger and draws excitement from it. The desperate need to set himself apart from the parents' lifeless sexual act leads to an omnipotent belief that he lives beyond the lawful limits of reality—namely outside the laws of both society and nature (Chasseguet-Smirgel, 1984; Ogden, 1999).

Stein (2005) argues that perversion uses sexuality as a means to control the other and to destroy intimacy, which is experienced as a threat. Perversion, in this sense, is using hostility and violence under a cover of love and care. The perverse subject has an extraordinary ability to arouse, excite, thrill and disturb the other. The "collar" by which this other is led is his own excitement. What is called "perversity", in the wider sense (Kernberg, 1995), is a strategic power used to divert the other from his or her path in such a way that, aroused and stimulated, he is tempted to collaborate, out of his own free will, in the perverse subject's project (Dorey, 1986; Khan, 1979). If the strategy is sophisticated enough, the seduction creates a sense of common self-discovery, or of desire originating in the seduced person rather than in the seducer's calculated strategy. Perversion is simultaneously an attempt to deny separateness, by means of creating a pseudo-twinhood—along with an attack on intimacy through the perverse refusal to allow any expression of his deep core. It is the attempt to penetrate the other without being penetrated (Parsons, 2000). It is, at one and the same time, a fake that seems truth-like, and a truth that appears as a fake. Stein believes that perversion is a specific matrix of relations, a sexual, paranoid, symbiotic and grandiose pact, an absolute yet hidden contract against reality. The perverse subject's pseudo-liveliness is, in fact, the massive silencing of a catastrophic primordial event which the self failed to survive (Stein, 1999).

The perverse subject's chameleon language

The scene of perversion is a scene of seduction. In this scene, which is shared, whether consciously or not, by two people, there is a continuous reversal of roles in which the chosen object, the person on which the perverse subject actually depends and with whom he yearns to fuse, turns from being the one in power into the one who is led, unbeknownst to him and sometimes against his own will, into the perverse labyrinth.

Whence does the perverse seduction take its power? How does the perverse subject go about the seduction scene? What allows him or her to recognise precisely the other's needs, and what enables him or her to so smoothly penetrate that other?

The perverse subject's accurate identification of the other's needs is not a true identification of the other's internal reality. It is, rather, a pseudo-identification which relies on his ability to adopt the other's discursive features in a way that prevents the other from identifying him or her as a stranger. The perverse subject's special gift is his extremely flexible and beguiling use of language. This is not limited to verbal language only but also includes the rich language of body gestures. Adopting the syntax of the other, the perverse subject actually employs it to trap and subjugate that other in order to neutralise the systems that identify him—sometimes even in his own eyes—as a stranger to that other, or as an outsider. In order not to be experienced as an-other, the perverse subject—like a kind of chameleon—espouses a range of nuances: syntactic, phonological and musical, as well as those involving mimicry, smell, dress, features of verbal and nonverbal language. This entire production has the aim of ensuring that the chosen other will not only fail to find out that he is under attack, but in fact will not register that he actually is in the presence of a stranger. In this sense he will be swallowed into a symbiotic discourse that negates the other and the world; object along with objectivity.[1]

Unlike in the case of pseudo-language—which adopts the other's nuances to create an artificial syntax so as to avoid intimate contact with insufferable contents—in the case of perverse language the other is not used only to avoid self-revelation, but also, and indeed mainly, to get the other to reveal himself without being aware of doing so. The perverse infiltration of the other is achieved by means of the false symbiotic adoption of that other's syntax with the unconscious or partially conscious aim to neutralise his defences. This is not a calculated, preconceived plan of action, but rather a survival pattern, programmed and mechanical, which the perverse subject has adopted at a very early developmental stage. The perverse subject is a child who has survived by virtue of his or her ability to decode the other's mental maps and to evolve extremely subtle identification and appropriation systems. This is a child who created pseudo-relations with a blocked object as a result of his ability to get in and out, to pick up a role and change it according to what he identifies as the other's wish or need. He achieves this by means of his ability to fill the other's vacant spaces without being felt or registered as a foreign body. Within the scene of perversion the other (the chosen object) does not only find himself responding to the contents that are being offered—contents that are experienced as surprisingly and movingly close to his own—but is also excited by the way of speaking, by the familiar syntax which the perverse subject uses as if it were his. The chosen object is in fact responding to a powerful illusion in which the things that are said to him seem to come not from outside but from within, namely to resonate his own interior. This illusion forms the very core of the system of perverse seduction. The above is closely related to what Stein (2005) argued about perversion as a simultaneous combination of falsehood that looks like truth and truth that resembles falsehood, as well as to what Chasseguet-Smirgel (1984) and Ogden (1999) wrote about the perverse subject's attempt to separate between truth and falsehood—which ends with the replacement of truth with falsehood, or the use of falsehood as a substitute for truth and life. Not only does perverse syntax "seduce" the other in order for the perverse subject to gain entrance—it also forces the latter onto the former. What is so powerful about the impact of this resemblance, this pseudo-twinhood (Stein, 2005), is exactly that it is unconscious both to the one who subjugates and to the one who is being subjugated. The effect can be compared to a metal object passing through a metal detector without being registered. In the scene of perversion the camouflaged metal object is the perverse subject's interest, whilst his "smooth" passing into the other's interior is related to the fact that the former is "wrapped" in a syntax that does not allow it to be identified as a foreign body. This is not simply a matter of a pleasant tone or an extraordinary personal charm, though these are often characteristic of the perverse subject. The mechanism at issue here is sophisticated and extensive—it creates for each chosen object an exclusive, personal syntactic code in terms of language, body and emotion. This is the key that opens the other's psychic safe, so there's no need to force entry. By identifying and adopting the psychic "fingerprint" of the chosen addressee, the syntax of perversion obtains a place in the latter's psyche with the aim of taking hold of it. Maintaining otherness, or observing the different within the identical, may at times become well-nigh impossible in the scene of perversion. The power of perversion, hence, inheres in that it touches on the wish to surrender (Ghent, 1990), to fuse.

In fact, one can say that perversion refers to those psychic areas where the other is rejected or emptied from his or her otherness. There is a huge as well as an essential difference between a reasonable amount of "chameleon-ness" which is performed in relationships on the basis of a psychic point of gravity that enables one to transcend oneself and search for the other's languages—and the perverse chameleon-ness which is performed in order to subjugate the other and annihilate his otherness. Perverse zones in a relationship constitute those zones where a psychic mother-tongue does not develop, and where chameleon-ness replaces the absence of a mother-tongue with an artificial capacity to use, in an indistinct way, any language.

One reason why the perverse subject is forced to infiltrate the other is that the primary object is experienced as impenetrable to the child. The only way that the child can penetrate the parent is by camouflaging himself in order not to be experienced as an-other. Thus, the perverse subject's chronic pursuit of a sense of danger relates not only to the repetitive infiltration of the parents' sexual primal scene, as Ogden and McDougall suggested, but also to the infiltration of the impenetrable parent him or herself. But even when the child infiltrates the parent successfully, injecting him or her with the child's own liveliness, the parent is still not experienced as being alive. This pattern repeats itself in later object relations too: the perverse subject is interested in conquest, yet whenever he makes one—the conquered object feels dead. This recurrent pattern is also expressed in language: The perverse person's infiltration of the other's language and his fusion with it doesn't create a vital discourse. The excitement remains empty, repetitive and meaningless, accompanied by a hollow sense of intimacy along with a sense of danger. The link does not evolve a common language in the natural sense, but rather a repetitive language whose seemingly common or shared elements are a poor compensation for its barrenness.

Laplanche writes about originary fantasies as relating to the origin of things: "As myths, they aim at offering a representation of what seems as enormous enigmas to the child" (2004, p. 55). This is especially relevant when we think about how the fantasy of penetrating the other through language turns sterile in perverse object relations: The originary fantasy in the context of language is the fantasy of entering the other's "body of thought". It is through words and discourse that we penetrate the inner mental space of the other and make it fecund. As Bion (1962a, 1962b, 1965) argued, the encounter between thoughts is impregnation (a conception). But when the originary fantasy meets a lifeless impenetrable object—the fantasy of impregnating the other by means of language becomes sterile, or becomes a fantasy about sterilisation. Behind the sexual excitation and the wish to impregnate the other, an experience of sexual and emotional relations as deadening will be concealed. Impregnation will be experienced as sterilisation. Thus, the perverse subject's language will penetrate that of the other only with the aim of fusing with and paralysing it, or in order to imprison it in a hollow, repetitious cycle. This is not just about the wish "to penetrate without being penetrated" (Parsons, 2000), but also about the compulsion to penetrate without impregnation, to penetrate in order to sterilise. Since injecting the other with the fluid of life does not lead the perverse subject to become full with a life of his own—he stays compulsively locked in the excitation of the injection scene and becomes addicted to it. The deep, unconscious reason why the perverse subject does not experience the other as being alive, is that he believes that what was injected into that other was a fluid of death—in a way that may resemble how he put to death the parental primal scene. With an inversion of both time and causality typical of the infant's unconscious—within the perverse subject's fantasy it is not the infant who was still born because the primal scene was dead, but the primal scene that was dead because the infant was still born. It is the infant who carries traits of death and infuses these traits into the scene from which he was created, thus reconstituting it as an execution rather than a life-giving scene. This perverse scene is re-enacted in later object relations, starting from the infiltration of the other in order to inject him with a fluid of life, and ending with the recurrent, tormenting confrontation with the inability to experience this other as really alive, a confrontation which time and again confirms the fantasy of the infant as being a source of death. McDougall (1978, 1982) relates to the perverse solution as a way out from the fear of a plunge into formless and infinite space. We may think of the perverse subject, in this sense, as someone who transgresses boundaries in order to feel them—or in order to feel that he has a hold on them. This strategy does not serve as a way of ridding oneself of a boundary experienced as suffocating or overly rigid, but rather as a way to protect oneself against experiencing the absence of any boundary that gives outline to the inner parts and holds them together[2] (Bick, 1968; Anzieu, 1989; Ogden, 1989a).

For the perverse subject, the primal scene constitutes the moment of his death as a subject rather than the moment of his birth as such. The frantic attempts to infuse this scene with life are actually meant to rehabilitate the subject as a living one. The infiltration of the language of the other, in an attempt to resurrect that other from within, does in fact reflect the perverse subject's real wish to get hold of an interior and to create a situation in which he can feel continuous and alive.

Perversion lacks both a concrete and an imaginary Third. In this sense, the primal perverse scene is not an imaginary scene between three (a mother, a father and a child who watches them or imagines them together in his absence) but a scene between two. The pervert's phantasy of the primal scene is a phantasy of a scene that takes place between a child and a dead object whom he conceives in order to be born. It is therefore an extremely hermetic and tight scene: one that not only excludes the triangle but also the very possibility of a Third, any possibility of otherness, of an exterior gaze or a perspective.

Clinical illustration

Joel, a married interior designer, is forty years old when he applies for analysis. He grew up in a boarding school, the only son of an aged couple, Holocaust survivors who never spoke about their past neither with him nor with themselves. His father was a remote and cold scientist who was hardly involved in his son's life. Joel was sent to a boarding school at the age of ten because of his father's academic career which forced him (and Joel's mother as well) to stay abroad for a relatively long periods. Without any close relatives that could help—there was no-one to look after him when they were away. Despite her frequent absences, Joel's closest relations were with his mother. One of his most powerful recollections was of her sneaking into his room at the boarding school after lights-out, stealing into his bed, and feeding him with candies. This happened whenever she came back from abroad, usually in an attempt to compensate for her absence, but Joel remembers similar scenes that took place also during school vacations at home. He remembers himself waiting for her impatiently, imagining what he will do to make her stay longer, always disappointed to discover how quickly those moments of warmth turned into periods of distance and absence. When he was about sixteen, his mother was diagnosed as suffering from Bi-Polar disorder. But he remembers long before that her bouts of depression, as well as his fear of returning home and finding her in bed. Sometimes she would lie down for weeks, staring at the white ceiling or alternately at Joel's face as at a white empty screen. There was, thus, an odd duplication between the "diurnal mother", that was often detached and alienated—and the "nocturnal mother" that was close and warm and offered forbidden pleasures.

As opposed to his father's masculinity, which Joel experienced as dull and blocked—his mother's femininity was experienced as very intense. In other words, in contrast to the father, whose sexual and emotional life was something that Joel couldn't even imagine—the mother starred in his imaginary life, featuring in vivid and seductive leading roles. Yet, there was something disturbing and arbitrary about his not being able to ever predict in what state he would find her, and what degree of closeness she would allow: will she hold him close to her breasts? Will she stare at him as at a complete stranger? Joel experienced the relations between his parents as lifeless and loveless. His birth, he claimed, was probably the result of a one night fault that never repeated itself.

Among his classmates he was always considered odd and he suffered from emotional abuse by older children during most of his childhood. At the end of his adolescence he moved abroad to live with remote family relatives. In those years he discovered his seductive force. He had an enormous number of one night stands with both women and men, never falling in love or developing any serious relations with any of them, but enjoying the sense of omnipotence and the fast turnover. In fact he caused both men and women to desperately fall in love with him—while he kept an interest in them only until the moment of sexual conquest. Then, in a minute, he would feel boredom and disgust. After three or four such years he started to suffer from sexual impotence, which prevented him even of the desired moment of sexual intercourse. He started to behave violently towards his sex mates, penetrating them with his offending words when he failed to penetrate them physically. Using the same talent with which he identified so accurately their weak spots in order to seduce them—he now identified their weakness in order to hurt them. The sense of power he drew out of their humiliation compensated him for the lack of potency, but at the same time increased his self disgust. At the end of this period he gave up both sex and love, and met his future wife with whom he has conducted a loveless marriage ever since. Despite his high intelligence and outstanding musical talents he makes his living as an interior designer in a small office, doing small design jobs which he describes as "banal and grey".

He applies for analysis, feeling that his emotional life is poor and that the only sexual contact he has is with himself. He compulsively masturbates in front of the computer, usually visiting pornographic sites, while eating sweets that harm his health. He chooses me as an analyst because, knowing me vaguely from the past and reading a book I wrote, he believes that we might share a "common language". It will take me some time to realise the symbolism of his wish to create a language in which neither of us would be a stranger. This illusion, which we both shared at first, cracked in the course of years of analytical work, when it became gradually clear to me that behind the rich, imaginative and colourful discourse a gaping abyss was lurking, and that the fine threads of seduction that he was spinning around me were meant to lead me to the verge of that abyss.

Something I could not put my finger on was happening during the analytic sessions. Joel cooperated, on the face of it, with whatever he imagined as *my* scenario of what analysis was all about: He lay down on the couch, brought in his recollections, his eyes filled with tears at the "appropriate" points. But while I was listening to him, I sensed he was eagerly awaiting any sound, any murmur from me; the mere twitch of a muscle. It was as though he allowed me to look at him while he was actually and simultaneously peeping at me, exposing me in a way which I was far from understanding. The analytic scene seemed to have all the necessary ingredients: aggression, sexuality, even tears, whose importance was that they fed into the illusion that the contents were not just brought into the analytic session, but were actually being lived in it. But what seemed to be a moving analytical scene—he was actually staging for my sake. I was the rapt audience to his performance. I was his captive. He chose whatever he felt was likely to interest me and performed it on the stage of the analysis, which has turned into a theatre stage. And he glanced at me, stealthily, in the course of the play, to check whether I was crying, whether I was moved, whether I liked what I saw, whether I was captivated. This was not where the trickery ended. Joel did not only conceal death by means of an illusion of liveliness—he also announced this death. He did not deny the truth, in this sense, but rather concealed the truth by means of the truth. When he applied to analysis, he said explicitly: "I came here because I feel dead." But this statement of the truth, too, was a falsehood, not in terms of its contents but in terms of its motive. It was a statement of the truth which came to serve falsehood rather than truth; a statement that served the false pact that he created with me, a pact in which this "truth" was a mere layer, a tool of seduction, not a goal. I felt simultaneously seduced—and weak. Tempted to follow—and in a danger which I could not even name.

In the course of one session, he brought a dream. In the dream he finds me lying on another couch, in another room, sleeping. When he wakes me up I say: "I dreamt that I slept with you". He lies down beside me but doesn't sleep with me.

I told him that through this dream he was describing a kind of "double couch". There was one couch on which he was "being in analysis", and there was another couch, in another room, on which there was an entirely different conversation going on. The dream reveals a wish to "wake me up", or to arouse me. But when he "goes to bed with me" (lies down beside me), he actually plants the wish in me: I am the one who says—"I dreamt that I slept with you".

Was he planting his wish in me? Or was I planting my wish in him? The dream shed light on the perverse exchanges that were happening between us, so subtle and fast that they were sometimes imperceptible. The perverse scene is always a double one, just like the double couch in the dream. In our double scene there was the analytical couch, the one on which he was laying and from which he conducted the analytical scene exceptionally well, and then there was another couch, one on which I was laying, one on which I was vulnerable. And I was vulnerable not only because I was asleep—that is to say, not sufficiently attentive to the fact that he was setting up a trap for me—but also because of my dreams ("I dreamt that I slept with you") and wishes which were apparently exposed to his gaze. The fact that he abstained from sex once he lay down beside me, and only let me dream about sleeping with him, was also connected with the fact that he avoided intimacy and preferred seduction.

This duplication made me think about the "double language" of Joel's mother. While she protected him, she also isolated him. She gave him strength, but only to keep him close to her. I started to wonder about how this pattern was enacted between us: in a way I felt that Joel was tempting me to take him into analysis not so that he may gain strength from it, but rather so that he may create with me a pact in which only mutual collapse ensures togetherness. This was not the togetherness of two living people, but the togetherness of the dead.

And indeed, a sense of exhaustion and boredom started permeating the analysis. Session after session I struggled with feelings of disconnection, difficulty in listening to or remembering what he said, with a sense of a pseudo-analysis in which we were locked together without a key. One day he told me that after the Holocaust his mother changed her name and refused to remember who she had been before. Joel had always felt that he had no access to what's "behind the scenes" when it came to his mother. I reflected on this living-dead mother, part of whom was cut off; on the fact that Joel was the only one who managed to enter her inner space. With his great gift of sensitivity, did he succeed in joining up with a loved one whom she had lost, thus entering a role she needed him to fill? Could his great success with both men and women also be understood as the enactment of that perverse, chameleon-like quality, the re-activation of his ability to adopt any language, to enter any role? One morning he woke up from a nightmare: his wife was being poisoned outside and he did nothing about it. He couldn't see what was really happening out there, but people reported to him that she was dead. I thought that he was telling me something about the early link between love and poisoning, perhaps even trying to warn me of what would happen if I became dear to him.

Joel told me that his parents never talked to him about sex. Yet there was a video cassette of his mother's that he found when he was about eight. It was a kinky video cassette that he took and hid. He was sure that she knew who took it, but she never said a word. I reflected to myself how he held his mother hostage by means of this video cassette which he hid and avoided her from asking back; how he also kept hold of her sexuality. Only at a much later stage he told me that his fantasy was that she and he used to masturbate in front of the same scenes.

In the session after he told me that he had suffered for a few days from a bout of depression. When we met again the next day he said he felt he had been manipulative the day before. He mobilised me so I'd worry. I said that there were times when pain came to cover up a kind of pretence, but there were also times when the pretence covered up an insufferable pain. He said: "Maybe that's the bigger danger. Not that you'll believe that it hurts when it doesn't, but that you'll believe me that I'm pretending while there's real pain". At the end of that meeting he said: "I always think about our endings in theatrical terms, like scenes in a play: is it the end of the scene? Not quite the end yet?" This was one of many shifts between falsehood experienced as truth and truth experienced as falsehood. When Joel said he thought of our meetings in theatrical terms, he actually meant that he was casting me in his drama, and that what guided him were not the rules of relationships involving two subjects, but the rules of theatre, involving a director and an actor, or an actor and audience. Whenever Joel succeeded to manipulate me he felt extremely powerful, but also very lonely. In this sense there was nothing he wanted more than turning me into this "object" that he manipulated, but at the same time there was nothing he feared worse.

In the course of another session he started on a very detailed description of how, as a boy, he would return home not knowing if he would find his mother in the kitchen cooking for him—or lying in bed depressed. Then he said:

> I told you once I could write a book about your humming and mumbling. But now I think we have developed a sort of joint humming thing. I notice that when I talk, you often hum, and I wait for it, it's like a confirmation, it's as though you're telling me—I am here, or—I agree with you, and I need that confirmation, I almost depend on it. I find it hard to go on talking when I don't hear it, because then it's as though you don't agree, or perhaps as if you don't listen.

I said: "If I don't make a sound you don't know where I am. You don't know whether I'm inside, lying depressed in bed, or waiting for you in the kitchen". Then he said: "But I noticed this too. When you talk I stay silent. I don't hum or mumble at you. I kind of don't let on what I'm thinking about what you say. I hold on to this sort of power position by not telling you what I think". This was the beginning of the explicit dialogue about our perverse pact. He told me, in various ways, how his frustration as a child became translated into a sadistic well-oiled control mechanism. He told me how in fact he was performing a kind of duet with me in which he left me hungry and anxious for his response while he coldly observed me. What was new here was that while he continued to manipulate me—he also drew my attention to, and warned me against, it. These were the first signs of a true pact—a pact whose centre was formed by truth. When he came in for the next session he announced that he didn't need the blanket that he used to cover himself with any more. I understood that if there was no blanket, no sweets can be hidden underneath. What he has given up along with the blanket was our imagined secret pact against the laws of analysis and against the world.

He was now able to tell me about an event in which he had sex with a man and a woman (simultaneously), saying that what made this event so exciting was not his being attracted to either the man or the woman, but rather the fact that he was desired by both of them. Then he recollected a family occasion in which he was a young boy and a stranger masturbated against him while he was in the man's room. He remembers feeling paralysed, unable to tell his mother who was waiting outside, an inch away, and didn't see. I said that it seems to me that he is not only telling me about the masturbating man but also about his mother's presence there. She failed to look after him, but her very presence, a mere inch away from this sexual scene, may also have been titillating, as though without being aware of it she was part of that scene; as though both she and the man were partners in a scene of which he formed the centre, just like in the sexual scene with the man and the woman he just told me about. The same question also held for me and him: Who was using whom? Was I looking after him or was I using him to arouse myself?

In the course of another session he told me that he saw me looking through the window when he arrived: "I saw you seeing me arrive. With this degree of closeness—do I actually need to knock on the door? If I forget for a moment who and what you are—I imagine you in the role of Solveig waiting for Peer, the man of her dreams".

I said: "Knocking on the door is like recognising the boundary. It's like saying—I am not Peer and you are not Solveig. But knocking would also conceal from me the fact that you know that I saw you arriving. That's exactly how this secret pact between us comes into being. I know that you know that I know, but we don't mention it. We go by the rules: you knock as if you didn't see me, I am surprised as if I didn't see you". He said: "There are millions of pacts taking place between us each time without you even being aware of them". And then he added: "Maybe we should decide that whenever such a pact emerges, it should be said out loud".

The perverse pact is always maintained through silence. In this sense, his proposal to call it by name constituted the beginning of his voluntary renunciation of this pact.

In our next meeting he told me a dream: he found himself in a hidden valley, watching a horse race. Suddenly he noticed a figure approaching him. It took him a while to realise it was a pig. He did not understand what the pig was doing there, but it looked at him so wise and sad that Joel, too, could not take his eyes off it. When I asked him about this dream he said: "The pig is a reflection of me". I said: "The part that you feel that is piggish is begging you to look at it".

Making the perverse pact explicit indeed brought out Joel's swine-like part. No more seductions, no more whispered spells. He no longer covered up anything from me. At times he addressed me as the basest slave or as a whore. During one session he said: "Do your job, sweetie, I'm paying you to work". And then: "I can't believe I am talking to you like that". I said—and meant it wholeheartedly: "I feel that you're begging me to fight for you. You say that if I don't—no one will". At this moment he broke into tears. And I could say that these were his first tears in years of analysis that I experienced as true. Not the sort of crying that was aimed for me to hear, but the kind that originated from within. I knew it because at that point, behind the couch, my eyes filled with tears, too.

Discussion

A few years after the end of his analysis Joel invited me to attend a breathtaking musical spectacle he produced on one of the alternative theatre stages. At the end of that evening he came to me and said: "I want to thank you. What we did together has a lot to do with what happened on this stage tonight".

Dimen (2001) says wisely:

> Not to concern yourself with what perversion means to a particular patient is, in fact, to enact a perversion of your own—to reduce your patient to a non-entity by annihilating his or her subjectivity, to confuse what the patient means to you with what the patient means to himself or herself, and thereby to violate the patient's (emergent) boundaries. (p. 832)

Perversion is operating against the perception of oneself and the other as singular beings. This is actually the worst derivative of the chameleon language: the annihilation of one's authentic inner colour. Analysis of perversion, therefore, has to attune itself towards singularity, towards one's unique colour, the one colour that is non-replaceable; the one colour that underlies all colours.

A part of the Holocaust's influence on Joel relates to his being the son of two parents that erased themselves as subjects of a historical and biographical sequence and as owners of a story that can be told and listened to. Not only the traumatic experiences themselves, but also the way in which they were erased, turned Joel's primary objects into empty ones. Is it possible that through the mechanical repetition of the sequence of seduction and abandonment Joel simultaneously created a compensating sequence—a story—but also emptied that story of any meaning? Did he enact, through the repetitive evacuation of every interaction, the emptiness which he perceived in both his parents? Furthermore, was his attraction to perverse interactions connected to the fact that the only moments within which he experienced his mother as alive—physically and emotionally—were the moments of her seduction of him under the blanket? In this sense, his fantasy of himself and his mother's joint masturbation over the same video-scenes was not associated only with sexuality as a way of keeping the mother hostage, as I thought at first. It was also one of the rare moments where he was in the position to peep into the bedroom of a living mother; of a mother whose sexuality—in spite of its entrapping perversion—proved that she was not entirely dead.

In a way, the moments of "emptying out" (usually after intercourse, but sometimes also after he succeeded in making his partners cry out of humiliation)—were the compulsive repetition of the experience of watching his mother's emptying out into the darkness time and again without being able to call her back. His sadistic control over his partners may be understood as a way to repeat the same sequence—this time with an omnipotent control that saves him from longing and pain.

Not surprisingly, this sequence repeated itself also in analysis. The staging of the dramatic scenes at the outset of the analysis served as a form of seduction and penetration. In effect, he used all literary and theatrical means not merely to conquer me, but also to prevent me from feeling conquered. The hidden aim of this staging was to keep me under the illusion that I was in charge of the process that in fact was going through loops and cycles. It was impossible to break the cycle until this pattern was enacted in the transference and the counter-transference.

Breaking the seduction pattern revealed the sadism and hatred behind the pseudo-love. It revealed the tricky duplication, re-enacted from within, between the dead mother of the day and the seductive mother of the night. But this exposure also made possible a more truthful, even if extremely painful, connection with both himself and me. Perversion, which until then would only erupt at night, was brought to light and exactly in that sense stopped rumbling beneath the surface of wakeful life. It became a truth that could be discussed, a truth that could be looked at.[3]

Dimen writes a lot about the combination of perversion and shame. More than Joel's perverse manic defence was built against the feeling of shame—it was built against the feeling that he had no uniqueness, as if none of his deeds carried or constituted meaning. Joel's chameleon personality enabled him to infiltrate everyone and everything— but at the same time fixated his self image as invisible, as no-one. In that sense it served as a two-edged sword: it filled him with sense of omnipotence on the one hand, but turned him into a faceless entity on the other. The challenge that his perversion presented analysis with was that of extracting his singular story out of the perverse scene's compulsion to repeat that story and annihilate its meaning through that repetition.

If psychosis is an attack on meaning—perversion may be understood as an attack on meaningfulness. It generates a pseudo-sequence where the hidden experience is of no sequence. It constitutes a repetitive continuum of events that revives time and again the pseudo sense of a plot—while the hidden experience is that of no story, of no plot, of going in circles rather than taking any direction or creating any shift.

Don't Tell,[4] a film which deals with the issue of incest, includes a charged moment in which the female lead, a young woman who dubs films, is working on a rape scene in a foreign film. She is dubbing the breathing of the raped woman and her stifled sobs as she watches the rape scene on the screen. Later it will turn out that this scene is a reconstruction of her own rape, as a child, by her father. The protagonist in this complex scene is simultaneously a witness to the rape of the other girl as well as the one who gives voice to this scene and translates it for others. She gives evidence or bears witness by the very act of providing a voice and a meaning to the unintelligible sounds in the foreign language. She does not know that like the girl on the screen, she too was raped. Thus, she is both witness as well as present at an event without a witness. She is a witness to the rape of the other and absent as a witness to her own rape. Like the young woman in the film, the perverse subject is simultaneously a witness to the other's event yet absent as a witness to his own. His gift for infiltration makes the other feel that he "bears witness" (to that other) so accurately that he could be said to be "dubbing" the other's interior, giving it both voice and meaning. Simultaneously, however, the perverse subject is absent as a witness who is subjectively present in his or her own catastrophic event. As a result of this absence, and due to his or her own emptiness, he evacuates any event to which he bears witness.

Corbett (2008), discussing sexuality, claims that static (sexual) norms impede our capacities to appreciate variance, to reflect justly, and to respond with empathy, even pleasure. But the perverse individual fails exactly in what this claim points at: pleasure, empathy and mobility. The perverse domain, thus, is not the one in which sexuality "diverges" from sexual current norms. It is the domain where sexuality stops being a playful area, a space for joy, for pleasure and self expression, and becomes a terrorising object in itself, an object which terrorises the self as well as the other. The indication of health does not lie in the mechanical obedience to social norms, but rather in the capacity to transgress those norms out of a reflective position that enables richness rather than frozen rigidity. Joel's perversion attacked exactly that: it created frozen rituals that dissociated him from his own vitality rather than expressed the uniqueness of this vitality.

In that sense, his analysis was about turning the meaningless, hermetic rituals into expressions of meaning. The spectacle he invited me to watch may have been his way of telling me that some of this did come true. That he gained the capacity to experience himself as a vivid plot that can be witnessed; that can be expressed in movement and words; that has music in it.

CHAPTER FOUR

The psychic organ point of autistic syntax*

Thinking autism

Not so long ago I was travelling on a train. Behind me sat a boy of about seventeen. As soon as he started speaking I realised that he must be located somewhere on the autistic spectrum. It was not because of *what* he said, at this point; it was the music of his speech, or to be precise: the absence of music. He was making one phone call after another, each consisting of the same text which he seemed to have worked hard to learn by heart: "how are you? How was it at work today? You sound a bit tired. When are we meeting?" This is how it went, again and again, in a metallic, flat tone. Then the train came to a halt and there was an announcement that there would be a few minutes delay. The boy got up, stood in the aisle between the seats and addressed me with huge anxiety. He wanted to know whether "a few minutes" meant five minutes or perhaps ten—and if it meant ten, then could it also extend into twenty?

---

*This chapter is based on the following paper, which won the 2011 Frances Tustin Memorial Prize: Amir, D. (2013). The psychic organ point of autistic syntax. *Journal of Child Psychotherapy, 39(1)*: 3–21. Reprinted by permission of Taylor & Francis Group (http://www.tandfonline.com).

The more concrete I tried to be in my explanations, the more anxious he grew: "So if you are saying that it might not exactly be ten minutes, then may it be eighteen? And if it could be eighteen or seventeen, then perhaps it could be fifteen minutes, too?" And then—this was the turning point for me—he said: "So nothing can be for sure". This is where I replied: "Don't worry. You'll see everything will come back". My words managed to calm him down until the train started moving. He repeated them again and again, always with the same intonation, without adjusting to the first-person: "You'll see everything will come back, you'll see everything will come back ...", until the engines started up again and the electricity came on.

The boy's use of words was in fact misleading. It seemed that their content calmed him down, and it is very likely that their content really played some role in it, but in fact he used those words in an autistic way, repeating them without any adaptation that might have turned them into his own. He did not say (to me or even to himself): "Everything will be okay, everything will come back"—but rather repeated my words without a single change, turning them through this repetition from vivid communicative signs into almost inanimate objects.

With hindsight I understood that his huge anxiety was connected with the fact that something in the repetitive, calming envelope had cracked. He probably took this train quite frequently and gained a sense of security and comfort from the regular announcements (which I noticed the he was reciting along whenever they were broadcast), from the fixed time schedule, from the fact that everything was known in advance. When this unexpected breakdown occurred the whole time schedule crashed, and worse, along with it crashed the text of the usual announcement whose regularity was so soothing. The one thing, at this stage, that could ease his anxiety was a promise that everything will come back and that order was going to be restored. For this boy, repetition acted like a pacemaker, a steady monitor which he needed in order to make sure he was alive. Clearly, what was at work here was a double mechanism: while repetition functioned as a pacemaker, keeping his life safe, it simultaneously kept him from liveliness; while it ensured steadiness, it would never allow either growth or transformation.

Autistic states are marked by the absence of an internal metronome or an internal pacemaker. When there is no such pacemaker, any upset is experienced as life threatening, a fall into an abyss from which there is no return. But what is the nature of this abyss? Autism, Tustin argues (1981), consists of a massive "not knowing" and "not hearing" which are the result of the traumatic and premature recognition of the infant's separateness from the mother. In her book *The Protective Shell in Children and Adults* (1990) she writes about the autistic child's delusional creation of a shell around him or herself through the idiosyncratic use of physical sensations, to the point of reaching a state of autistic encapsulation. Though encapsulation suggests a sense of shell-like protection, the autistic child has no such experience whatsoever. The physical motions he or she uses in order to create the shell around him or herself are random, fragmented and temporary and do not add up to an ongoing sense of being enveloped. The first differentiations in regular early development are between "comfortable" and "uncomfortable", "pleasant", and "unpleasant". Soft is pleasant. Hard is unpleasant and uncomfortable. A sense of soft becomes gradually associated with "taking in" and acceptance. Sensations of hard are tied up with invasion and forced entry. At a certain point these sensations become associated with the baby's bisexuality. While harsh penetration becomes "male", soft enfolding becomes "female". When during breastfeeding, the hard nipple and the soft mouth which takes it in are in collaboration, what occurs is a "marriage" between female and male principles. If, by contrast, no integration between hard and soft occurs, and the child becomes locked up in the hard for the sake of protecting the soft which remains inaccessible, a situation arises in which the male and female principles rather than cross fertilise, clash with one another or become mutually alienated. This is the autistic condition[1].

One main feature of autism is the absence of any sense of place and time. An autistic child has no sense of what is between two objects— whether these objects are feelings or things—or of what must be crossed in order to get to know them (Hamilton, 1992). Hence transitional objects or acts are absent in autistic development. Even a simple act such as thumb sucking, which can be observed in the womb, requires a moment of suspension—until the thumb reaches the mouth. Unlike the tongue, the thumb is not inside the mouth to begin with. It must cover a distance, a movement that also extends over time, in order to get there. It is exactly this suspension that the autistic child cannot bear, since it compels recognition of separateness and of distance, and requires an ability to endure frustration.

For autistic children, hard autistic objects or soft confusional objects (Tustin, 1990) replace transitional objects and acts. The autistic delusion is that the hard things "block the hole", which has come into being as a result of premature separation, and that they prevent hostile materials from entering or leaving through it. The confusional objects, in contrast, stop the bleeding and absorb the seepage of fluids. These pathological objects have a survival value because they keep the threat of death at a safe distance and compensate the child for what he believes he has lost. But since they are put to an idiosyncratic and compulsive use, the objects form an obstacle to psychological development.

One notable feature of autistic objects is that they are used in a manner that does not coincide with their original function. The children use them in idiosyncratic ways. From a practical point of view, the child uses the object in a meaningless way, but from his own point of view it plays a crucial role in defending him. Not only does the child use these things without any relation to their original function, but there is no imagination in the way she or he handles them either. ·

Imaginative play always involves an as-if quality and a certain awareness of the physical separateness of the object. But the autistic child's use of the object is ritualistic, rigid and intense, and lacks the as-if quality as well as the quality of separateness. In this sense, Tustin argues, autistic objects resemble fetishistic rather than transitional objects. No fantasy seems to attach to them, and if it does, it must be a raw type of fantasy, one which is very close to physical sensation. Due to this paucity of fantasy, the uses of the autistic objects remain repetitive and uniform. The objects remain static in the sense that they lack the unlimited qualities that lead to the development of new associative networks as happens in imaginative play. Another typical feature of autistic objects is that they lack distinctiveness. A similar object (creating the same feeling in the hand) can always replace a lost one. The autistic child's use of objects does not take into account their symbolic meaning or their practical functions. It focuses on the sensual element of their form only, namely their outline and the sensation it affords.

In this same vein, we can say that on encountering two words with the same phonology, the autistic child will not be able to differentiate between their meanings. The same goes for rhymes. They "touch" the ears and the eyes in similar ways, they make the same feeling inside the mouth, and therefore they are experienced as identical. So the autistic child's tendency to repeat words or to create endless chains of rhyming words is not a type of word or rhyme play. Rhyme and wordplay are evolved forms of expression, which a person uses when he or she has a sense of physical separateness from other objects. The autistic child, however, has no ability for verbal play. Her use of words is identical to the use of autistic objects. For the autistic child, objects are not the substitute for the missing person, but the person him-or-herself, or part of them, since they yield the sensation the autistic child is yearning for. In the same way, words are not a substitute or a symbol but the thing itself. Words don't hold meaning, argues Tustin: they are a shape inside the mouth, a sense of something on the lips, an imprint left·on the tongue's surface.

The word "yearning" is not actually adequate to describe the autistic child's relation to the object. The autistic object serves to avoid the need to yearn for satisfaction or to bear frustration. That is why the autistic child needs that object, but never really yearns for it. Providing immediate satisfaction, the autistic object will not allow for any lingering between expectation and fulfilment. This lingering, if the person is able to stand the tension it generates, is what brings about the ability to engage in symbolic actions like fantasies, memories and thoughts. While the autistic child, who avoids this lingering, survives physically—her psychological-cognitive development will remain extremely limited.

Derek Ricks' research on the development of psychotic language (1975), cited by Tustin herself, shows that those children never displayed the universal sounds of babbling typical of normal language development. By skipping crucial early stages of play, like the stage of normal babbling in infancy, or that of thumb sucking when the baby creates a simulacrum of the breast, the child actually loses the critical creative work of developing anticipatory fantasies, which serve as a necessary bridge to reality (Winnicott, 1958). Instead of the ability to imagine what is physically absent, the child uses autistic objects to separate between herself and reality in a way that blocks the possibility of sharing this reality with others. Alvarez (1980) discussed, in this context, the way in which autistic children transform living words into dead ones which serve to block communication.

When sensibility and sensuality are directed at objects instead of human beings—rather than becoming regulating and adjusting—it becomes stereotypical and excessive. This is why where in normal development thumb sucking arouses a rich life of fantasy and imagination—in the autistic child's development the thumb becomes the whole of experience and the absolute goal. I will return to this in the context of the autistic inverse use of the psychic "organ point".

Because autistic objects are rigid and lifeless, they are likely to crack beyond repair under pressure. Unlike living people, who can heal and change, their rigidity makes autistic objects irreparably vulnerable. This irreparable fissure is the source of the primary despair of the autistic child as well as of his or her rigidity in the face of change.

Living in a world of inanimate objects, the autistic child has no sense of recovery as a vital and spontaneous process. Unfamiliar with the existence of living creatures he or she is unaware of the natural processes whereby damaged tissue may heal without manipulative intervention. Such a child has no grasp of the natural processes that go on independently of him or herself. Understanding the notion of recovery does not merely release the child from the responsibility of having to mend the crack, it also opens an entire repertoire of human gestures such as forgiveness, understanding and empathy. This extends the concrete and narrow repertoire of retaliatory as well as reparative acts. This extension introduces the possibility of hope and compassion. As a result the child stops oscillating between states of vegetative unconsciousness and states of torturous hyper-sensitivity.

Tustin (1981) argues that as much as the notion of interiority develops—namely an element that is invisible and cannot be touched but which can hold things together and connect between them—a concept of "mind" evolves which is related to imperceptible events like thoughts, fantasies, imagination and memories. In primitive states, the mind is experienced as a real container that prevents things from falling apart. Autistic children never develop a sense that their mind can hold things together. Their excellent memory is in fact a déjà-vu experience: whenever a formation occurs that is reminiscent of another, earlier and significant one—the experience is of a situation happening anew.

Donald Meltzer (1975) speaks in this context about autistic children's difficulty in attaining a three-dimensional experience of the object which is required for creating the function of containing. To feel that the object is a container with the capacity to hold pain, we must experience it as three-dimensional. At the same time, in order to internalise it, we must also perceive ourselves as three dimensional. Within two-dimensional relations the object is experienced as inseparable from its sensory features. Autistic children actually cling to their objects: They touch the people around them continuously and inappropriately since in their experience people exist or are present only through contact with their external surfaces. Adhesive identification, namely the defensive clinging to the object, serves to lessen the anxiety of breakdown. Autistic children don't experience themselves as three-dimensional just as they don't experience others as such. Their self, too, is experienced only in terms of its external features and not as having an interior. Neither the object nor the self are experienced as having a space that may contain pain. As there is no interior it is both impossible to internalise objects as well as to think them. This is the reason why the autistic child can easily and mechanically repeat sentences—without understanding them or containing their meaning.

In his chapter on "the autistic-contiguous position", Thomas Ogden (1989a) writes that the attempt of patients who are in this developmental position to create "a sensory floor" may express itself in physical activities that create a muscular demarcation, or else in autistic forms of self-soothing behaviours like humming, foot tapping, hair twiddling or earlobe fondling, etc. Their trying to adhere to the surface of another person is an attempt to revive their own surface or to create a temporary illusion that their own surface is intact. By adopting facial expressions, gestures or intonations of the other, they are trying to stick parts of the other's surface to their own, unstable one. The act of imitation is an attempt to restore the foundation which is necessary for any self experience. Since in the autistic-contiguous mode the experience of being penetrated is equal to being perforated and torn, imitation is the one non-harmful option since it allows the other's influence to be carried on the external surface rather than being internalised.

In her paper "The problem of empathy: bridging the gap between neuroscience and psychoanalysis toward understanding autism" (2009), Judith Mitrani focuses on the contribution of neuroscience to the understanding of autism and on the relations between psychoanalytic formulations of autism (mainly Tustin's, Bion's and Meltzer's) and the scientific findings concerning two important phenomena, the first of the two is that of the "mirror neurons": since these neurons are thought to be linked to empathy and to language, and are also thought to provide a mechanism for action-understanding, imitation-learning, and the simulation of other people's behaviours—their dysfunction, namely the phenomenon of "broken mirror neurons" (Ramachandran & Oberman, 2006), is thought to be linked to autism (see also Rizzolatti et al, 1996; Iacoboni et al, 1999; Baron-Cohen, 2003). The second phenomenon is the "salience landscape theory", that is thought to explain other symptoms of autism, for example repetitive motions such as rocking to and fro, avoidance of eye contact, hypersensitivity, and aversion to certain sounds, all symptoms that cannot be explained by the mirror neuron hypothesis. Research findings point out that when perceptions—for example, sights, sounds and smells—are processed by sensory areas in the brain, information is relayed to the amygdala, which acts as a portal to the emotion-regulating limbic system. Using input from an individual's stored knowledge, the amygdala determines how the person should respond emotionally. Messages then cascade from the amygdala to the rest of the limbic system and eventually reach the autonomic nervous system, which prepares the body for action. Autonomic arousal, in turn, will feed back into the brain, amplifying the emotional response. Over time, the amygdala creates a salience landscape. Autistic children are thought to have a distorted salience landscape, perhaps because of altered connections between the cortical areas that process sensory input and the amygdala, or between the limbic structures and the frontal lobes that regulate subsequent behaviour. As a consequence of these abnormal connections, any trivial event or object might set off an extreme emotional storm in the child. This hypothesis is thought to offer an explanation as to why autistic children avoid eye contact and other novel sensations that might trigger an insufferable upheaval of emotions. Salience landscape theory appears also to provide an explanation for the repetitive motions and head banging seen in children with autism. Researchers seem to be onto the idea that self-stimulation somehow dampens the child's autonomic storms. According to Ramachandran & Oberman (2006), salience landscape theorists believe that such distorted perceptions of emotional significance might explain why many autistic children become preoccupied with trifles such as train schedules, while expressing no interest at all in things that most children find salient (Mitrani, 2009).

Since UCSD's two-theory explanation for the symptoms of autism—mirror neuron dysfunction and distorted salience landscape—are seen as complimentary, researchers believe that it is possible that the same event that distorts a child's salience landscape also shuts down the mirror neuron systems. Alternatively, the altered limbic connections are thought to be a side effect of the same "event"—whether genetic or environmental—that triggers dysfunctions in the mirror neuron system.

But scientists have yet to identify which genetic and/or environmental factors actually lead to the development and functioning of mirror neuron systems and which of these factors may prevent their development or impede their functioning. The same goes for factors that can lead to a distorted salience landscape or those that aid in the development of one that is relevant and true. Mitrani suggests that we might think of this situation as a virtual möbius strip, where neural systems needed for interaction with the environment are disabled, and the interaction with the environment necessary for further neural development becomes increasingly deficient.

The point of Mitrani's paper is that if Tustin is right—that children prone to autism cannot bear to be aware of otherness and therefore cannot tolerate true interaction with others, and that their idiosyncratic, auto-sensuous behaviours function to block out any awareness of otherness—then the broken, deficient or dysfunctional mirror systems may occur as a result of these addictive behaviours that distract attention away from the perception of otherness. It might be, Mitrani further suggests, that these mirror systems were at one time turned on, but the autistic child's subsequent prolonged engagement in auto-sensuousness functions (as a result of relating to a depressed or pre-occupied emotional environment that was too much to bear) actually shut the mirror systems down. When auto-sensuousness replaces mental and emotional activity, keeping out unwanted or insufferable stimulation and happenings, the baby may become enclosed in an impoverished environment. This could certainly result in stultification of cortical development and truncation of neural connections, furthering isolation, and so forth. Mitrani suggests that if the mirror systems are shut off or broken and the neural activity that would ordinarily allow a child to understand intentionality is absent, one might wonder if, when the autistic child's auto-sensuous behaviours are interrupted, could it be that he or she suddenly finds him or herself in an incomprehensible and therefore frightening world where seemingly ordinary events are experienced as extraordinary. Is it possible, then, that new or extraordinary happenings are instinctively anticipated as so very threatening to the survival of the relatively inexperienced child, that they are massively blocked out of awareness and thus might appear (to the observer) to go unnoticed by the autistic child? If so, this might be a valid explanation to the distorted salience landscape that is typical to autistic children and adults (Mitrani, 2009).

Autistic syntax as an inverse use of the psychic organ point

Autism is not a single entity caused by a single reason, but a rich phenomenon which may probably express itself through many variations.

I would like to address now the specific features of autistic syntax, both intrapersonal and interpersonal, which seem to be typical to all variations. The musical notion of an organ point will serve as my point of departure in explicating how autistic syntax transforms what was supposed to function as a substrate for linguistic polyphony into a one-dimensional, repetitive score that is void of feeling. Within autistic syntax, the human characteristics of both self and other are denied, turning the other into an autistic object which blocks, with his or her concrete presence, the hole created by his or her own absence. The resulting discourse is one that either imprints its forms on the other's language or rubs against it as against a surface, but never creates a living dialogue. Within the autistic discourse repetitiveness replaces cross-fertilisation, thereby annihilating the ability to create or to allow anything new as such.

In tonal music, the notion of an organ point refers to a sustained tone, namely a stable fixed beat which appears typically in the bass. The organ point usually begins as one of the musical chord tones, but unlike the other tones which change incessantly, it continues playing, inevitably creating a dissonance with other chords where it sounds "foreign". Organ points have a strong tonal effect, pulling the harmony back to its roots (Barrows, 2000; Frank, 2000). This is, in fact, the groundwork from which the musical tissue evolves: the sustained tone creates a kind of baseline, a backbone or a centre of gravity which allows the generation of the polyphonic texture.

The autistic condition could be described as one within which the organ point is dissociated from the musical piece itself. Here the strong tonality of the organ point does not pull the harmony back to its roots, but severs the former from the latter, thus changing its status from foundation to centre, from constituting the background to being a dominant, exclusive presence.

In her paper "The hollowed envelope" (2007) Naama Keinan refines the discussion of Andre Green's (1988) notion of negative hallucination in a manner that may further elucidate the autistic use of the psychic organ point. The crux of Green's theory, claims Keinan, is the moment in which the infantile subject becomes able to negate the mother's presence so as to turn her into a background screen onto which his or her own representations may be projected. The negative hallucination, hence, is a framing structure, the white screen necessary for representations to appear. For this framing structure to evolve, the mother must be fully present, thus allowing the infant to erase her and to create the representation of her erasure. But a mother who is emotionally absent will not enable such an erasure. In that case, instead of a void as a framework, a terrorising void emerges which entails an ongoing need for concrete sensory adhesion. In other words, when the normal process of erasure is not feasible, then in lieu of the negative hallucination, of the "white" as a screen or as a frame for thoughts, what occurs is a partial or complete annihilation of thinking as such. Bion (1965), in a similar context, distinguishes between "nothing" and "no-thing". The no-thing plays the same role as the negative hallucination which generates the framing structure within which an image can emerge. Symbolisation and thinking rely on the no-thing since the absence of the object invites reverie. "Nothing", by contrast, is a psychic area marked by emptiness and cessation, an area that can neither allow nor bear representation.

The inverse use of the psychic organ point is actually a similar phenomenon, in which what was meant to be the framing structure refuses to be erased, to fade and take the status of background. In autistic states, the absence of an integrated and stable psychic organ point prevents the creation of a polyphonic flow, thereby reducing the entire "psychic music" into a uni-dimensional score. Instead of affording a base for flexibility and renewal—the sustained organ point becomes a dominant, exclusive content.

Let us get back to actual music for a moment: since the unchanging tone of the organ point is foreign to the various chords which it joins as part of the musical piece, each time it "interferes" with a chord, the sensation yielded by the chord becomes less clear and distinct. This is actually part of the ambivalent magic of organ points—the magic on account of which they simultaneously pull the harmony towards its roots, while also engaging in a game of familiarity and strangeness with it. Returning to the autistic state in this context, one could say that because the harmonic root in the autistic state is weak and unstable to begin with, any deviation from or intervention in its harmony is experienced as destructive. The autistic condition lacks sufficient capacity to preserve the inner harmony and resonance, a capacity which would make the temporary dissonance bearable. Instead, what characterises the autistic use of the psychic organ point is that it causes it to dominate the entire harmonic and melodic flow. The autistic state actually erases harmony, preserving the organ point as a single-beat score, which allows neither revival nor flexibility, and which holds out an illusion of stability by means of repetition. What is hereby expropriated from the psyche is music. In this sense, autistic experience can be seen as an "inverted use of the psychic organ point".[2] This kind of use removes the polyphony from the psychic music, turning it into a texture that lacks both volume and meaning.

Suzanne Maiello (1995) suggests that the sound of the mother's voice, alternating with silence, may give the foetus in the womb a proto-experience of both presence and absence. It is a fact that the maternal voice introduces an element of discontinuity in an environment that is otherwise characterised by continuity. At times the voice speaks and at times it is silent. It is an external object as unpredictable and uncontrollable as the breast will be after birth. Both the voice and the breast alternate moments of presence and moments of absence, which are not always in harmony with the child's needs and can therefore be a source of both well-being and frustration. These background sounds cease abruptly at the moment of birth; the child is suddenly deprived of the most constant and familiar part of its sound-world, in which the maternal heart-beat possibly has both a structuring and a calming function, corresponding to the role of the regular and repetitive bass beating the time in music.

Maiello claims that the foetus's proto-mental nucleus hypothesised by Mancia (1981), which is capable of transforming sensory information coming from external objects, could use the mother's voice for the creation of an internal object with sound qualities, which in turn could become the ground on which rests the preconception of the breast. The absence of the voice on the other hand might give the child a proto-experience of emptiness, of the emptied space in which thinking and language will develop and serve as instruments for re-evoking—namely "giving voice again"—to the lost object by naming it. Maiello describes a young patient whom by singing loudly or shouting with rage during the session, was trying to get control of the "bad absent sound-object" that she felt to be threatening her from inside. The "good sound-object", on the other hand, would have been safeguarded within the melodies and words of her songs. Much as Maiello's patient uses sounds in order to regain control of an absent object—the rigid autistic use of the psychic organ point can be understood as a desperate effort to get hold of an absent inner pace-maker which had not—or could not—develop and be internalised.

The function of the psychic organ point in autistic states is reminiscent of obsessive-compulsive thinking: a repetition that is void of emotional meaning and which has become a mechanical mode of surviving. Keeping the psychic organ point as the only text, thus—evacuating polyphony from music—is similar to keeping repetition as the only psychic activity and emptying that psyche of reach, creativity, and life.

This evacuation takes many forms within autistic language. In order to understand them the various components of language must first be mapped. Tustin often spoke of the autistic child's difficulty in integrating the hard and the soft. In the present context, we can regard the rules of syntax as the hard part of language, since they represent the rigid and unchanging rules of speech. Similarly, we can consider feelings, humour, irony, musical intonation, and everything that fills this syntax with singular individual meaning, as the soft parts of this language. Since in the autistic condition, as Tustin argued, there is a strong split between the hard and the soft parts, and no way of linking between them—the zones of autistic language may be considered as the ones in which language often generates syntactically accurate but emotionally barren discourse. Although the contents of this discourse may lend themselves to understanding, it neither reaches the "soft tissues" of the other nor opens up so that the other may penetrate the soft tissues of the speaker him-or-herself. People with autistic encapsulations are often capable of a proper syntactic use, but it is usually accompanied with emotional rigidity and a sense of hollowness. Thus, this syntax[3] does not create an emotional dialogue although it produces an understandable speech.

A patient of mine used to talk incessantly of Bach's "The well-tempered clavier", demonstrating an extraordinary knowledge. His verbal text was fascinating as far as expertise was concerned, but remained emotionally flat and barren. It was quite obvious to me that what fascinated him was not music—but rather the mathematic analysis of its constructions. He clung to the hard parts of the music score—namely the musical syntactic rules—but remained detached from the soft parts, namely music itself. In a similar way, another young patient used to describe in detail her deeds during the day that preceded every session. Those deeds were described in a very elegant language, but one that lacks an emotional soundtrack. Here, as well, the incapacity to integrate the soft and the hard created a language that combined a perfect use of syntactic rules—along with a massive attack on emotional linking.

The encapsulated child's lack of language is an extreme mode of staying within the soft internal tissue without making contact with the outside. This releases the symbiotic fixation from the need to meet reality and from the flexible motion that contact with reality requires by its very nature. The autistic child locks out the "not-me" by creating a world in which the other plays no part and has no significance.

For autistic children, language is a form of auto-sensuousness in the same way that words serve as autistic objects and autistic shapes. They can lean or rub themselves against them, but they cannot use them in order to communicate. This is why autistic children prefer consonants, which are felt more clearly in the mouth. Similarly they will be attracted by rigid forms of rhyming, due to the identical, repeated and invariable sounds it creates, offering them a rigid surface against which they can lean or rub themselves. The difficulty to perceive time and space, as well as the inability to perceive the other as a whole subject, prevents the creation of a language that can bridge the gaps of time, space, and otherness. Autistic language, much like post-traumatic language, exists outside of space and time, abolishing otherness and thus erasing the gaps that are a crucial condition for the urge to create language. The autistic use of words does not allow for shared meaning, nor does it allow for meaningful discrimination. For the autistic child words are frequently an agglomeration and agglutination of tactile shapes and objects that function to block out the awareness of difference and similarity between two lively entities, rather than an acknowledgement of and an attempt to communicate with other human beings, since in order for connections to be made, separateness must be tolerated (Mitrani, 2009).

Much like they hide their tongue in their mouth and their excrement in their rectal sphincter, autistic children hide words inside their mouth or deposit emotion within the word which closes tightly around it until it is no longer accessible. Words are locked within their syntax or non-syntax. To the same extent, meaning is locked inside the word with no way out. Unlike in functional language where meaning is hidden in the word or stored by it—here, rather, it is "held" in the word as in a fist. Indeed, autistic children refuse to release their words much like they refuse to release the grip of their fist. Even before refusing to enter a conversation with an-other, they refuse to engage in a conversation with themselves as other, namely to acknowledge the fact that things have an external objective existence and thus may be open to symbolisation and representation. The autistic relation to words much resembles the special use of autistic objects. It is not only non-conventional but also devoid of meaning. Autistic children add the word to themselves as though it were a hard "piece", thus treating it as a concrete object: not as a signifier of a live part of the body but as an artificial body part. This is the reason for words' immobility as well as their repetitive and rigid use, which yields no new associative movement.

An autistic adolescent patient used, for instance, to begin every sentence he uttered with the last part of my previous sentence, creating an identical sentence in an inverse order. Thus, when I said to him: "Something bothers you today", he answered: "Today something bothers you". If I told him: "It is hard for you to choose between the two" (colours, for instance)—he answered: "Between the two it is hard for you to choose". This pattern sometimes generated fascinating combinations, but most of the time produced repetitive sentences that were not meant to promote communication but rather blocked it. In some ways this pattern resembles the phenomenon of regurgitation in babies. Language, for this boy, was not a vivid, changing texture that produced new nets of associations. It was rather experienced as a collection of dice which he gathered and scattered again and again without letting himself undergo any change as a result. Autistic language does not allow one to linger within or with something, nor does it afford a place to be in.

How does autistic syntax express itself within interpersonal relationships? What is an "autistic dyad"?

What I call an autistic dyad does not only refer to an original dyad between mother and infant. An autistic dyad is actually what emerges between the autistic encapsulations of two people. It may also occur between partners, between siblings, or between patient and therapist. In this kind of dyad both partners are erased as subjects. Not only does the interpersonal syntax within the autistic dyad deny representation, but the dyad itself may come to supplant representation, and hence representational language, by allowing one person to use the other as a barrier against both the external and the internal world. The dyadic language which is generated as a result is one that is founded on the compulsive sealing of surfaces instead of on the creation of meaning, and therefore creates two—rather than three—dimensionality. Having expropriated the other's subjectivity, one uses that other, or parts of the other's presence, as though it were something by means of which she or he can fill holes. The lack of perception of the other's human features, in fact, is so serious that the other him or herself can be made to serve as the "thing" that fills the hole opened up due to his or her own absence. And so the other in this dyad can simultaneously be the missing person, the hole that opens up as a result of his or her absence, and the object that fills that hole, without letting this mechanical chain of events create any psychic trace. Schellekes, in her paper "The dread of falling and dissolving" (2008), writes that the fusion of the autistic encapsulated person with the environment creates an illusion of the object being part of the self and serves as a defence against separation which is tantamount to a sense of psychological death. In the same context, Keinan (2007) writes that the "twin object" may at times yield an experience of "reproduction" within which the subject feels safe. This type of relationship of dense fusion, as Bick (1986), Gaddini (1969), Meltzer (1975), Tustin (1986), and Mitrani (1994) described it, is typically bereft of a sense of three-dimensionality and of the presence of an internal space for mental processing. In this situation there is no gap between subject and object—a gap that is crucial for the development of mental space (Schellekes, 2008). Indeed, Tustin herself underscored the autistic child's aversion to the state of two-ness and the effect he or she can have upon the environment while avoiding this reality. For example, echolalia is often reinforced by the parents and caretakers, who feel compelled to repeat what they say to the child many times, just in order to get his attention. Thus, they are forced to go the child's autistic way (Mitrani, 2009). Tustin described how:

> Mother and child become autistic objects for each other, [living] in a sensation-dominated cocoon in which they fit each other predictably and perfectly. They become each other's ecstasy. [...] a beneficial feature of the bearable lack of fit of the good-enough mother is that it provides a space in which chance happenings can occur. Such chance happenings are agents for transformation and change. (Tustin, 1981, p. 119)

Tustin cautioned that:

> The mother and baby who become entrancing autistic objects for each other and fit each other perfectly, prevent the possibility of such a space. This means that the child's mental development is massively stunted and goes awry, because agents of change are shut out. (Ibid.)

The deep refusal that marks the autistic dyad is the refusal of the new. The only way to survive, for both partners, is by means of repetition.

This repetition maintains the sense of friction between the surfaces—and as such, the sense of being—while avoiding the possibility of its leading to any new experience and to the creation of an-other or otherness. Friction, within autistic dyads, replaces penetration much like repetition comes instead of the possibility of fertilisation. In this type of dyad one partner serves as the other's organ point. Because of the rigidness and dominating quality of the autistic organ point, the autistic dyad cannot transform into a polyphonic one and remains two dimensional: a dyad of two organ points that each generates a static and parallel melodic line rather than intertwining to create a rich and vital musical texture.

In a beautiful chapter dedicated to the nature of aesthetic judgment, Donald Meltzer and the literary scholar Meg Harris-Williams consider the way in which the individual psyche adjusts itself to the aesthetic object (Meltzer & Harris-Williams, 1988). In the encounter between self and object, they argue, two modes of contact are exposed: "carving" and "enveloping". It is between these modes of contact that the drama of the inner world finds its symbolic form. The foundation out of which the psyche emerges is the interaction between the infant's psyche and the mother-world's bodily spaces. On this basis all developmental thought processes evolve (1988, pp. 186–187). In other words, every encounter with an external as well as with an internal object involves the "crossbreeding" of two mental functions: the function of carving, which is responsible for the revealing of the strange and the new, and the function of enveloping, that is—the function of containing what is carved within the firm walls of continuity, causality, and memory. It may be said that what is severely missing in the autistic frame of thought is, in this sense, the ability to integrate carving and enveloping. The refusal to the new is so rigid since there is no ability to envelope what was carved or to carve what was enveloped without the total collapse of the sense of "I-ness".

Clinical illustration

When Naomi, an autistic young woman, begins psychotherapy, what strikes me most is her bizarre response to my words. She relates to them in a sensual way—rather than verbally or symbolically. She rubs against them, tastes and chews them, but never "thinks" of them. This turns our entire discourse into an uncanny one, like a walk through an unknown terrain in which the usual rules of reality or even those of inner reality do not obtain.[4] She does not anticipate what I am saying as a listener, but rather like an animal waiting to pounce on her prey: she closely follows the motions of my lips, the sound of my words; she sniffs the intervals between them, "swallows" or "laps up" what I say in the most concrete sense of these terms as though they are foods, sweets, a bitter pill. She never adds anything of her own. Instead, she repeats what I say with my exact intonation. Her eagerness to hear my words does not seem related to what they actually mean but rather to the very contact they enable her with me. It seems connected with the simple physical fact that I am talking to her, that my lingual surface is there, stable enough to let her rest her own lingual surface against it. She is not trying to "swallow" my words as a primitive form of incorporation. Rather, she treats the words themselves, especially the consonants and the vowels within every word, as inanimate objects which she scratches against her tongue, chews or spits out. Alvarez (1992) writes about the moment in which she understood that Robbi, an autistic patient, was experiencing one stimulus in terms of another: a voice (an auditory stimulus) in terms of a colour (a visual stimulus). Naomi experiences my voice in terms of taste. There are "tasty words" against "bitter words that you must swallow". No logical link can be identified between what she experiences as tasty and the word's objective content. These idiosyncratic bizarre differentiations are connected more than anything else to the relation between consonants and vowels within every word: a multi-consonant word is experienced as tasty, while a word that has more vowels is experienced as "bitter" or "disgusting". Multi-consonant worlds that rhyme are the tastiest. It takes me a while to realise that we have created a kind of autistic dyad, using a seemingly common syntax whose meaning remains hidden. I utter a word and she returns it to me after she tastes and chews it. I am deluded, for some time, by the thought that these exchanges are playful, deriving a great pleasure from what I understand as an achievement of a common private language. But as opposed to other secret languages—I discover, mainly from my counter-transference reactions, that this secret language does not encode any meaningful content. On the contrary: It annihilates meaning, replacing it with an empty syntax that blocks any possibility of understanding or being understood. My emotional presence is blocked too. Naomi treats me as a fluffy surface that can be ignored or passed through. If I "give her tasty words" she gazes at me for a moment, hoping for more. Otherwise she detaches herself, or gazes through me. More and more often I feel that what seems like a speech which is directed at me—or a game that she is playing with me—is actually an autistic act that is aimed to block any recognition of my separateness, as well as any possibility of creating living relationships with me.

Naomi is the eldest daughter of three. During her mother's pregnancy she suffered a severe stress which finally caused a premature delivery, one month before the anticipated date. Naomi was born with the umbilical cord wrapped around her neck, barely breathing, and remained hospitalised for two months after her birth. The mother suffered from a psychotic depression after Naomi's birth, refused to see her or hold her and was convinced that the baby was "Satan" who was born to destroy her. Following an intensive psychiatric treatment, the mother began to recover and started taking care of the baby, but was not allowed to be alone with her until Naomi was one year old. The father, a hard worker, was usually absent for most of the day and was not available for either his daughter or his wife. The only person who steadily took care of Naomi during her first year was the grandmother (the mother's mother), to whom she was deeply attached. When Naomi was about one year and a half the grandmother had a severe stroke (in the course of which she fainted in front of her little granddaughter), after which she was hospitalised in a rehabilitation institute and never regained the ability to speak. Following the event, Naomi's mother went through another period of major depression. At the time of the grandmother's stroke Naomi already spoke a few words and was physically developed and active. A few months after the event her parents noticed that she became introverted and withdrawn, that her language did not develop properly for her age and that the few sentences that she did say sounded bizarre both in shape and in content. She was ascribed to a special school for children with communication difficulties. At school, too, she was quite withdrawn. Her mother, who gave birth to twins (a boy and a girl) when Naomi was four years old, felt relieved when Naomi shut herself in her room and preferred that she would not demand her attention. Whenever she did try to play with her Naomi used to cling to the mother's body in a very disturbing manner, arousing fear and disgust in her. On her 12th birthday Naomi lay down on a train track, waiting quietly for the train to come and simply "take her away from there". She could not say (not then, not in retrospect) anything about this except that this "there" was not pain, or loneliness or anything else with a name, a form, or content. "There" was the region which was not "here". She was then referred to a behavioural psychotherapist and stayed with him for almost eight years. The treatment ended when he moved to another town and she was then referred to me.

The idiom "there" repeated itself through many years of treatment. I noticed that in many instances Naomi said "I am there" while she intended to say "I am here" (for example, whenever she entered my clinic). In many instances she asked me to "come and sit there" while she actually wanted me to come and sit close to her. Interestingly, Alvarez describes a moment of progress in Robbi's treatment when he was finally able to make a wish to be "there", namely when he could imagine a place that was not "here and now" (Alvarez, 1992). In an opposite manner, what I felt with Naomi was that there was no "here" that was available for her. While Robbi could not hold in mind the possibility of "another place"—and could only relate to the concrete and the actual—Naomi could not have any vivid experience of the "here and now". She was "there", detached from any living company or common experience.

"There" is a zone of neither life nor death, neither past nor future, hence not a living present either. "There" is what will never be "here". It is an outside zone, from which both psyche and body have been evacuated. In this sense, the autistic existence is a capsule which is neither psyche nor soma, a region which denies any possibility of assimilation. Autistic language does not constitute a representation of the physical or the sensory but rather turns into a barren form of sensuality, a type of sensuality that is expropriated from the senses.

For a long period of time during Naomi's analysis I felt as though I was walking through a swamp, a dense, sticky space in which words stretched sideways, became kneadable, bounced or were thrown back and forth—but never created discourse. At times I felt as an object myself, which Naomi, unbeknownst to herself, was throwing back and forth. Between sessions she used to send me repetitive, meaningless text messages, as if she were using me to fill up the hole which I myself created by being absent. All this was accompanied by a strange sense that whatever was happening between us was not happening "here", that is, in a breathing, vivid present.

How do we turn "there" into "here"? How do we turn the annihilating use of the psychic organ point into an emotional polyphony? Suzanne Maiello quotes Novalis who writes beautifully: "Disease is a musical problem. Cure is a musical solution" (Novalis in Maiello, 1995). If a rigid organ point is a musical problem—what is the musical solution?

The reclamation of psychic polyphony

Tustin (1981) frequently mentions the moment of therapeutic shift as expressed in the autistic child's ability to draw a cross or to make a cross-shaped move (either in the form of a body movement or by means of an act). Crossing means connection; it means entrance into and exit from; it means two lines in motion that create a joint texture, one which includes a point of contact but also leaves intact the singular direction of each line. The cross indicates the stage at which an ability to integrate the hard and the soft, the inside and the outside, begins to form. Until they arrive at this stage, autistic children have no sense of their interior and all they can do is relate to surfaces. Thus, for example, they experience the front part and the back part of their body as separate and distinct. Being able to join them depends on the critical notion of interiority, the space that connects between those parts.

In language, too, we can think of the act of "crossing" as an encounter between two, oppositely directed lines, or between one thing and its opposite. A sentence like "x is both hard and soft" is, in this sense, a "cross sentence". Parallel lines, which Tustin describes as characterising autistic drawings, are infinite since they never intersect. In language, parallel lines can be manifested in using words without conjunctions, or in stating something without the concomitant awareness of its possible opposite: there is only "soft, soft, soft" or "hard, hard, hard", without any qualification, dilution, or intermixing. Since the recognition of opposites has a potential of putting a limit—but also a potential of creating a link—a cross sentence would be any sentence in which something that was only "either or" becomes "both and". To revert to the earlier musical context: polyphony is a musical form of crossing. It is the transition between parallel musical lines to musical lines that cross.[5]

What, then, is crossing within the interpersonal syntax?

In the interpersonal discourse or syntax, crossing would be any encounter that involves recognition of difference and separation; any interaction that is not a kind of friction with the other's external surface but a dialog with his or her interior, in a way that relies on the recognition of such an interiority as well as on the understanding that such an interiority is always singular: an-other in its very essence. It is the ability to acknowledge the other's singularity that transforms the discourse with him or her from being a friction-less motion of parallel lines to a crossing encounter with an-other; not with an-other featuring as a silent surface lacking any spontaneous movement of its own, but with an-other as a body with substance, real and alive.

Alvarez (1992) believes in the therapist's emotionally active parts facing the emotional lifelessness of the patient. She does not recommend concrete deeds but emotional ones, namely adding an emotional "sound-track" to the detached, mechanical and lifeless acts of the autistic patient (Gampel, 2005). In working with states of autistic syntax, it is the aim of the therapeutic intervention to create within the therapeutic relations moments of emotional crossing, moments that actually constitute a polyphonic texture—initially within the relations between patient and therapist and subsequently also within the patient's relations with him or herself. The critical therapeutic transition, thus, will be from using interpersonal discourse as a means against development—to using it as a lever for change; from using the psychic organ point against psychic polyphony—to using it as a foundation for the polyphony of relationships and of the internal world.

During the long years of therapy with Naomi, the "crossing point" which I could identify was reached when she was able to tell me, spontaneously, that she hated the colour of my shirt even though it suited me. This moment involved not only her recognition of my separateness (she can hate something that I love) but also the crossing of her sensual surface experience (green is a bad colour) with the recognition that this experience does not constitute a universally valid truth (green may be a bad colour for her shirt but a good one for mine). Not only had crossing occurred between the experience of "me" and that of "not-me", but something vital in the here and now was formed as a result. This moment was preceded by many years of a frustrating struggle to create a living contact and a meaningful dialogue with her. Besides my ongoing stable presence—it was my insistence on her finding "words of her own", my refusal (though tender and gradual) to cooperate with her repetitive demand to create endless meaningless chains of words, and my insistence on being the owner of my thoughts (and on her being the owner of hers)—that finally turned us from two "captives" into a free thinking couple.

If the rigid use of the psychic organ point constitutes the problem—the solution should be oriented towards insisting on polyphony, or rather towards creating psychic conditions that enable polyphony. Naomi reacted in an autistic encapsulation to a situation in which—besides an extremely traumatic birth—she experienced a violent separation both from her grandmother, to whom she was deeply attached, and from her mother with whom her initial bonding was extremely fragile. Her clinging to the sensual aspects of words instead of creating them as agents of meaning—was related to the fact that the "sound-floor" she generated that way protected her from fragmentation and from being violently penetrated by the outside as well as by her own feelings and needs. The autistic dyad she formed with me created a situation in which we stayed "side by side" without being connected—and therefore without acknowledging our separateness. In a certain sense, her unconscious intention was to create a scene in which I was "glued" to her (through her repeating of the sounds I made) without acknowledging me as a separate subject. Her clinging to me (much as her clinging to her mother's body) was an effort to adhere to my surface without enabling a link between our interiors. The serious therapeutic mission, therefore, was to enable the connection between our inner worlds—hoping that the inner connection would gradually soften her need to glue our surfaces. In order to create such a connection it was not only that my own inner world had to be present, but that her own inner world had to be invited in too. This process began with my refusal to cooperate with her endless uninterrupted sound chains, which strengthened the illusion of a common surface, and continued with my insistence to bring myself into the room in a manner that would not allow the continuous gluing of our surfaces as a substitute to relationships. In musical terms it can be said that I insisted on creating, on the basis of Naomi's rigid organ point, polyphony of my own—inviting Naomi to also create one herself.

One of the most touching illustrations of this process was when one day she brought in a special recording machine (that she received from her school for a special task she had to fulfil) which could create an echo of what was just recorded. For example, having recorded "how are you?", the machine would create an endless loop of "How are you? How are you? How are you? ..." until we recorded something else—which also repeated itself endlessly until we interrupted it with a new one. Naomi was extremely fascinated by this instrument and was willing to listen to the loops of her voice for the whole session. The endless repetition calmed and rocked her and she listened to it with her eyes closed. At a certain moment I suggested a game in which I stopped abruptly the loop by recording a new sound of my own, inviting her to do the same, to surprise me, to change. Naomi protested at first and was furious with the unexpected interruption, but very slowly, she was carried away. What was recorded eventually was an orchestra of both our voices: High pitched, low pitched, asking and laughing. This beautiful musical texture, which Naomi called "our orchestra"—was the first proof of her ability to create psychic music.

Following the therapeutic sequence in retrospect I can trace the shift from the autistic dyad—in which there was a massive ignoring of our being separate subjects—to the partial recognition of my otherness as well as a new capacity to enjoy it. It might be said that what made the change was my paced interruptions to Naomi's autistic sequences. I now understand that those moderate interruptions created both an elastic envelope and flickers of surprise, serving simultaneously as signs of my separateness and as signs of my stable presence.

Bollas (1987) suggests a beautiful distinction by which the self, rather than being a stable structure, is a kind of interior grammar, a regulatory process which he calls "the un-thought known". What he points out is not an unconscious content, but rather an unconscious structure, namely a collection of regulatory processes which together constitute the essential pattern that characterises each and every individual. Thus, we can consider "autistic encapsulations" (Tustin, 1990), "black holes" (Eshel, 1998; Grotstein, 1990) and "hollowed envelopes" (Keinan, 2007) as regions devoid of an interior grammar or a unifying and regulatory interior syntax. This regulatory syntax is replaced with a psychic organ point that generates a mould whose function is to supply the illusion that the diverse parts of the self are held together but without a sense of ownership and subject-hood. Naomi's therapeutic process was a process of restoring the subject to the object, of putting life into the lifeless. It was a process whereby the psychic language (intrapsychic as well as interpersonal) was transformed from a fixed mould into a live content, from a "wall" into a "place", from that which blocks speech and thinking to what enables the experience of "being here" and "being within".

CHAPTER FIVE

The inner witness*

The "inner witness" is a mechanism that develops as a reaction to a reasonable experience of infantile helplessness and the maternal impingement that results from, it along with the presence of a sufficient experience of a Third,[1] concrete or imaginary, that is internalised as an inner observer. This mechanism becomes crucial to the subject's capacity to shift between the first-person and the third-person of experience, or between the "experiencing I" and the "reflective I"—and has an essential role in maintaining a continuous sense of being as well as in coping with trauma.

Three types of testimonial narratives will be differentiated here in terms of the presence and magnitude of the function of the inner witness within their syntax: The first testimonial mode is one within which the function of the inner witness is accessible, and therefore the shift between the first-person and the third-person of experience is possible. As a result, an imaginary shift between the voice of the victim and the voice of the witness is enabled, yielding an inner space. This

*This chapter is based on the paper: Amir, D. (2012). The inner witness. *International Journal of Psychoanalysis*, 93: 879–896. Reprinted by permission of John Wiley & Sons Ltd.

testimonial mode involves a work of representation and the creation of new meaning, thus producing a testimonial narrative within which the traumatic events are not merely repeated but also undergo transformation. As against the first testimonial mode, the second mode remains a first-person mode of report. Unable to shift between the voice of the victim and the voice of the witness—it produces a text that preserves and enacts the traumatic memories and the traumatic features, and is thus characterised by the same sense of isolation, fragmentation, disorientation, and lack of coherence which are also typical of the traumatic experience itself. In this sense, the second testimonial mode illustrates the very materials to which it testifies. To sharpen the distinction between these two modes: the first mode is one which enables the shift between the first-person and the third-person of experience, while the second mode is located in the first-person only. This does not necessarily refer to a testimonial narrative that literally uses only the first-person, or that is characterised by an excessive use of "I" within its text, but rather to a testimonial narrative that uses no distancing so as to maintain a living continuum with the traumatic memories and, consequently, also with a sense of selfhood. Lacking any reflective attitude, it enacts the traumatic experience without being able to turn it into an integrated narrative, incorporating it without being capable of transcending it. Actually, within the second testimonial mode any transcendence is experienced as a split between the subject and his or her identity.

As against these two testimonial modes which do preserve a certain link with traumatic memories, there also exists a third, "psychotic mode" of testimony. This mode attacks every possible link with the trauma, separating between the subject and his or her memories as well as between the subject and his or her own sense of selfhood. The "psychotic testimonial mode", which will be the focus of this chapter, annihilates the capacity to turn the traumatic events into any sort of narrative and it does so by inhabiting the very creation and use of communicative language. Completely lacking the function of the inner witness it is founded neither on the ability to shift between the first and the third-person of experience (like the first mode), nor on the capacity to stay exclusively in the first-person (like the second mode). In fact, it destroys both the first and the third-person and thereby the very existence of an experiencing subject. This mode of testimony actually joins the traumatic "Real" without being able to distance itself from it on the one hand and to create a vital link with it on the other.

Every testimonial narrative includes a specific interaction between these three testimonial modes, and this interaction has significant implications for recovery: when the meta-structure of testimony is predominantly in the first mode—while the second and third feature in it as secondary modes—the resulting narrative will be capable of organising itself around the traumatic experience, preserving the necessary distance to enable both reflection and symbolisation as well as the creation of new meaning. On the other hand, when the meta-structure of testimony is predominantly in the second mode—the resulting narrative's capacity of containing the traumatic materials is poor. This testimonial mode does not enable reflection and thus preserves the traumatic memories mainly through repetition. The metonymic sequence of the second mode is interspersed with regions marked by the third, psychotic mode, but rarely shifts to the first mode.

When the dominant mode is psychotic—trauma turns into what I call a "negative possession": a psychic condition which prevents both the representation of traumatic events as well as the ability to preserve meaningful and vital contact with them.

Trauma is a term we tend to use in a vague and often confusing fashion, meaning both the cause of the pain (the traumatic event) and the consequences of it (the traumatic reaction). Even when we point to the traumatic event itself we may still confuse early traumatisation with adult trauma or cumulative trauma with massive trauma. Each of these traumatic domains has its different characters, but they are also interconnected in diverse ways, as I will further demonstrate.

Developmental cumulative trauma

Winnicott (1965) employed the metaphor of "holding" to denote the total environmental provision prior to the initiation of object relationships. Essentially, it refers to a specific developmental period he labelled "absolute dependence". If everything goes well during this particular phase, the infantile ego undergoes significant internal development, changing from un-integrated states to a more structured integration. In the phase of absolute dependence there is no desire. Only later, with the infant's growing awareness of his or her dependence upon the mother, it is accurate to speak in terms of meeting desires. When things go well during the period of holding—the infant has no means of knowing what is being properly provided and what is being prevented from impinging. By "gross impingement" Winnicott means that which interrupts the infant's continuity of being. Impingement can be either traumatic or strengthening. If the infant has a good-enough ego-support from the environment—he or she will gradually learn to meet the impingement, which will result with the strengthening of his or her self awareness. But if the impingement is too early or too intense, the result will be traumatic. The reactions to impingement happening over a period of time cause damage to the personality and result in fragmentation and a threat of annihilation (Winnicott, 1953).

Masad Khan (1964) elaborated on the effects of cumulative trauma on the mental apparatus, claiming that when repeated adversity breaches the individual's capacity to maintain emotional equilibrium, symptoms or character distortions emerge. Cumulative trauma begins in the period of development where the child needs and uses the mother as his or her protective shield. Since the healthy infantile growth requires a basic minimum of reliability of this function, the inevitable temporary failures are not only corrected and recovered from but also provide nutriment and stimulus to new functions in growth. It is only when these failures are significantly frequent, leading to a pattern of impingement on the infant's psyche-soma integration, that they set up a nucleus of pathogenic reactions. The breaches in the mother's role as a protective shield lead to a premature and selective ego-development: some of the emergent autonomous functions are accelerated in growth and exploited in defensive action to deal with the repetitive impingements, while complementarily the disturbance of sensory and motor development prejudices the normal evolution of libidinal phases. Instead of a separate and coherent ego-structure integration, multiple dissociations take place intrapsychically. As adults, these patients have but little capacity for quiet getting-alongness. They must keep themselves engrossed, tantalised, stimulated, or they fall into a most apathetic sort of non-existence and unbeing.

Piera Aulagnier (2001), discussed in detail in the second chapter of this book, addresses the absence of the father from the discourse of the "word-bearer" (the mother), the impingements of the mother's unrepressed death wish followed by her refusal to allow the infant his separate existence and his own thoughts, and the "identificatory void" caused by the mother's inability to provide historical and emotional context for the preverbal experiences inscribed in the infant's body—as crucial traumatic factors that may foretell psychotic potentiality or psychotic development. The expression of such psychotic potentiality will be manifested as "holes" in the child's memory and discourse: an incapacity to create a coherent narrative of his or her own.

The reaction to early traumatisation, as we will further see, resembles in many respects the reaction to adult trauma. One of the main similarities between the two types of trauma relates to the inability to bear witness.

Trauma and testimony

The psychological and psychoanalytic literature dealing with trauma refers extensively to testimony and to the major role of the other in bearing witness to a trauma the victim often has not, and could not have, witnessed him-or-herself. Writers from various theoretical fields (Laub & Auerhahn, 1993; Oliner, 1996) describe trauma as something that has taken place "over there, far away", an event that does not belong to the "experiencing I". Survivors of trauma claim that they live in two worlds: the world of their traumatic memories (a kind of everlasting present) and the real world (the concrete present). Usually, they neither wish nor are able to integrate these two worlds. As a result, the traumatic memory is preserved frozen and timeless, and psychic movement becomes automatic, aimless, and senseless. Wiseman and Barber (2008) refer to this as "the music of knowing–not knowing" which passes through generations of survivors. Caruth (1996, pp. 91–92) writes about the "traumatic paradox" in which the most direct contact with the violent event may take place through the very inability to know it. Trauma is not only an experience, she claims, but also the failure to experience: not the threat itself, but the fact that the threat was recognised as such only a moment too late. Since it was not experienced "in time", the event is condemned from now on not to be fully known (Caruth, 1996, p. 62). Van der Kolk (1996) argues that while terrifying events may be remembered extremely vividly, they may equally resist any kind of integration. These memories remain powerful but frozen, un-transformable by either circumstantial processes or the passing of time. They are subject to neither assimilation nor developmental change since they are not integrated into the associative network. Liska (2009) writes in relation to the topic of literary representation of trauma:

> For decades, literary approximations of silence determined the poetics of Holocaust remembrance. This poetics assumed that only

silence can truly render what occurred and convey the horrors of this past in a language uncontaminated by inadequate discourse. Since the ultimate witness, the dead, are silent and speak only through the living, it is silence itself that is summoned. Only silence itself, the interruption of communicative speech, the empty space between words, the self-erasing trace of the non-representable, the open wound of the abyss, the caesura, the rupture, the stuttered, stammered word approaching silence is true. (Liska, 2009, p. 151)

Yolanda Gampel describes in her book *The Parents Who Live Through Me* (2010²) the permanent co-existence, typical of Holocaust survivors and other victims of institutional violence, of two "background images": one is a "background of security" and the other is a "background of the uncanny". According to Gampel, children who were in the Holocaust witnessed the sudden erasure—physical as well as emotional—of their parents, and were often left with alienated parental figures, frozen and lifeless. As a result, a background of uncanny (1999) emerged. From that point on, this background will be the receptacle of all loss and will function, simultaneously, as a means of denial, likely to express itself in the form of "psychic holes" (Gampel, 2010, p. 33). Traumatic experiences are not transformed into a personal narrative: they are primary impressions that lack a verbal representation. Ferenczi (1921) relates to trauma as a total experience in which the object failed the child either through an action or through the inability to act. As a result, the infantile subject is put to death through a split: since she or he no longer exists—they feel neither pain nor worry as to the possible loss or destruction of their body. Recovery from trauma may occur only within a healing relationship which allows traumatic memory to transform into narrative recollection (Ferenczi, Abraham, Simmel, & Jones, 1921). Laub (2005), in a paper entitled "Traumatic shutdown of narrative and symbolization", quotes Moore (1999) who argued that we cannot know that the traumatic event has taken place until an-other supplies it with a narrative. A person can know his or her story only when he or she tells it to what Laub calls, "his or her inner thou" (internal other). But since trauma causes a critical injury to both the internal and external other, that is to say, to the addressee of any dialogical relationship—it ruins the possibility of an empathic dyad in the inner representation of the world, leaving the subject with nobody to address, either within or outside him-or-herself. This catastrophic loss of the good object compels the victim to internalise the only available object, the aggressor him-or-herself, as a "malignant selfobject" (Kohut, 1971) with whom she or he identifies. In *Remnants of Auschwitz*, Agamben (2009, p. 139) argues that the process of witnessing occurs in the space between the survivor who has a voice but nothing to say, and the "Muselman" who has much to say but no voice. Shoshana Felman, in *"Testimony"* (Felman & Laub, 1992), writes:

> That 'something happened' in itself is history; that 'someone is telling someone else that something happened' is a narrative. In many respects, a narrative is also a historical proposition, much as history is also the establishment of the facts of the past through their narrativisation. (Ibid. p. 93)

The traumatic event, although real, takes place outside the parameters of "normal" reality, such as causality, sequence, place, and time, claim Felman and Laub (1992). This fundamental absence of categories lends it a quality of "otherness", a salience, a timelessness, and a ubiquity that puts it outside the range of associatively linked experiences, outside the range of comprehension, of recounting, and of mastery. To undo this entrapment in a fate that cannot be known but can only be repeated, a recovery process involving the construction of a narrative, the reconstruction of history and essentially, re-externalisation of the event has to be set in motion (Felman & Laub, 1992, p. 69). This is the core of bearing witness.

The inner witness

The psychic circumstances that prevent someone from being able to bear witness to him or herself are the outcome of an early traumatisation which destroys the capacity to create a frame of reference in which he or she may experience themselves as being coherently comprehended by others. This kind of traumatisation is not characterised by any temporal or spatial contours. It is rather an ongoing process that bars the subject even from recognising the fact that he or she is taking part in a catastrophic event. The absolute absence of the psychic function of the witness results from the fact that something within one's history deprives him or her of the capacity to feel their own exclusion: there is no inside outside of which one can dwell. There is no stable or solid substance from which one can be expelled. Indeed, there is no way to be expelled from expulsion, or excluded from exclusion.

Survivors of trauma live through complex relations between "being a victim" and "becoming a witness". While it may seem obvious that a victim constitutes the most accurate witness—this assumption is far from truth. In fact, not only are the reciprocal relations between being a victim and becoming a witness far from obvious, but being a victim often annihilates the ability to become a witness. This tension between the position of the victim and that of the witness also exists, regularly, within the primary mother–infant dyad. Here, the function of the inner witness does not only develop, as can easily be assumed, as a result of the maternal capacity to bear witness to her infant, that is to validate, through her attuned witnessing, the infantile first-person (the infantile I); it also results from the infantile experience of being a victim of the mother's inevitable "primary violence" (Aulagnier, 2001), namely the verbal and physical actions meant to take care of the baby—but also causing him or her to experience helplessness. As Piera Aulagnier (2001) claimed, some primary violence is normal and even necessary for building that part of the ego which constitutes meaning. However, an excessive amount of it becomes what she calls "secondary violence", which is violence in itself. In a developmental sense, the helpless infantile situation (caused by the maternal primary violence) triggers the establishment of the inner witness, owing to the necessity to move away from the victim-like situation towards an ability to observe and to endow it with meaning. The function of the inner witness enables the infant to survive the inevitable primary violence through the ability to bear witness to him or herself in a situation that basically excludes him or her as subjects with a will. This function defends the coherence of the self in a situation where the infant is denied any space of choice. Thus, the inner witness develops as a reaction to a reasonable experience of helplessness and in the face of a sufficient experience of being seen by a Third. An optimal measure of helplessness will orient the child towards the concrete or imaginary Third and will allow him or her to transcend the victim-like situation through adopting and internalising the function of the witness implemented by this Third. The function of the witness may be seen as the experience of the observer within the observed. It is the freedom to transcend the limits posed by the body and reality constrains into the ability to create an inner narrative.

In situations where this movement is not possible, helplessness does not activate the function of the witness but rather annihilates it altogether, destroying not only the option of a third-person (an inner observer) but also the option of a first-person (an "experiencing I"). In terms of the psychic syntax, excessive helplessness annihilates the first-person, while the absence of a Third annihilates the third-person. Since the function of the inner witness involves the ability to shift between first-person and third-person—here this function is either severely damaged or does not develop at all. The earlier and the more powerful the damage—the more harm is done. In certain situations we deal with an extremely fragile inner witness, while in others this function has never emerged in the first place. The latter situations resemble autistic or psychotic states in many respects. The inner witness is not a specific internalised object, but rather a specific internal function, which is in charge of the unique shift between two psychic positions: the position of the victim and the position of the witness.

In his article "Objectivity, subjectivity and the triangular space", Ronald Britton (1998) suggests that the primary triad is what enables the child to acquire an archetype of object relations of a third kind, within which the child is located in a position of an observer and not of a participant. In that way, a "third position" is created within the infantile self, which enables the child to enjoy the point of view of the other while also preserving his or her own (ibid. p. 42). The function of the inner witness can be seen as a derivate of Britton's third position,[3] one which concerns the specific capacity to cope with trauma and traumatisation: it is not merely the function which enables the shift between the "experiencing I" and the "reflective I", but the one in charge of the shift between the position of the victim and the position of the witness. In that sense, the inner witness is associated not only with the ability to observe oneself, but also with the ability to bear witness to what is observed, namely to validate one's subjective experience. In courtrooms, the witnesses are often the ones who tip the scales. Their testimony is what determines the sentence. The absence of the inner witness therefore means the absence of the sentencing or determining function, which either negates or confirms the subjective experience. In the absence of an inner witness the subject will develop an inner syntax that keeps a narrative sequence on the one hand, but preserves this sequence as non-valid on the other. The sequence therefore can be reversed at any moment as well as negated by anything and anyone. Within the analytic relationship, these will be the patients who incessantly wonder whether they bear witness to something that really took place or whether they are inventing and rewriting their own history.

The destructive implications of this experience are huge: if the inner witness is experienced as a false witness, this cannot but doom the subject to a false sentence. If the inner witness is experienced as hostile, it will persecute the subject from within. But an absent witness condemns the subject to annihilation.

Felman (1992), discussing Camus' *The Fall* (1956), suggests that the erasure of testimony, imposed upon the protagonist (who observes the fall of a woman from a bridge but does nothing about it), causes the gradual fragmentation of everything that until then seemed safe to him. The unconscious refusal of testimony, namely the refusal to let an event be a part of one's narrative, is a defensive reaction with fragmenting consequences. The reason lies in the idea that the very act of testimony is crucial to the work of psychic construction. The witness in *The Fall* actually sees the woman before her fall and hears the sound of her crashing body after he has already passed through— but does not witness the fall itself. He misses it. Felman writes in this context:

> This *nowhere* from which the other's voice has at the same time reached and failed to reach his ears will henceforth lie in wait for the narrator *everywhere*, as the obsession of a vocal echo [...].
> (Ibid. p. 169)

Camus' protagonist becomes an obsessive witness who cannot separate between what is and what is not his, between what cries from within and what cries from without. Having refused—albeit unconsciously— to be a witness, turns him into a witness to everything. This obsessive witnessing is, as will be discussed later, one of the main features of the absent inner witness.

Within the three types of testimonial narrative distinguished earlier the third one is the one of which the inner witness is completely absent. Its absence generates what I call "a psychotic syntax", based upon a relation of "false equality" in which there is a total symmetry between me and not-me and between inside and outside. In the very same way, no fixed subject-object relations exist within the psychic syntax: the object can act upon the subject, or remain subject-less. The thing one holds can in fact hold him or her. It is not simply the event that constitutes testimony, but rather the testimony that constitutes the event. This certainly refers to what Matte Blanco called "the unconscious symmetric relations" within primary thinking processes

(Matte Blanco, 1975; Rayner, 1981): while most relationships that can be discriminated are "logically asymmetrical", namely relationships whose converses are not identical to them (for example: a is to the left of b, has the converse: b is to the right of a)—the unconscious usually treats asymmetrical relations as symmetrical (for example: a is to the left of b, will have the converse: b is to the left of a). Logical thought, whose functioning is virtually synonymous with secondary thinking processes, usually entertains propositions about asymmetrical relations. Symmetrical relations, on the other hand, are characteristic of primary thinking processes. The conception of a whole object and a part of it always involves a conception of space or time relation between them. For example: if a includes b then b is included in a. This of course uses asymmetrical logic. But when symmetry intervenes, the conception turns into: a includes b and b includes a. When symmetry rules, whole objects are experienced as identical to their parts. Similarly, in ordinary logic when we discriminate that event b follows event a, we will also recognise that a precedes b. But if symmetrical logic intervenes, b follows a as well as a follows b. When this applies succession is not distinguished, there is no time sequence, and time as we know it actually disappears. Not only that asymmetrical logic is essential to the possible recognition of, and thoughts about, the external world—but the very idea of "external" is logically asymmetrical since it has the converse "internal". Thus, without the ability to use asymmetrical logic there will be no discrimination between inside and out (Matte-Blanco, 1975; Rayner, 1981).

The psychotic syntax that is generated by the absent inner witness points to the fact that the function of the inner witness serves both as a membrane that separates inside from outside and self from other—and as a barrier dividing between asymmetrical and symmetrical logic. Its absence annuls any possibility of hierarchy or individuation, causing the above mentioned fusion of inside and outside, and of cause and effect. This psychotic syntax may appear as a reaction to massive adult trauma, but is more likely to appear in reaction to early cumulative traumatisation, as the following clinical illustration describes.

Clinical illustration

Gabriella, a young woman in her thirties, applies for analysis as a result of a vague distress. For the past eight years she has been studying for her first degree, unable to complete her duties. She reports repeated failures in meeting deadlines, keeping her assignments, sifting what's important from what isn't. She reports many affairs with both men and women, but describes them in an undifferentiated and dispassionate manner. The way she speaks about her life leaves a sense of hollowness and meaninglessness. Although her linguistic capacity is rich and words are abundantly available, her discourse feels evacuated, uprooted, and seems to lack any point of gravity.

Gabriella is the eldest of two daughters. She describes her father as almost absent during her childhood, a weak, ignorant, unfaithful and infantile man who never took any responsibility for his family, whether as a father or as a spouse. The mother, a depressed and violent woman, used to humiliate him, particularly in Gabriella's presence. She remembers her mocking his low intelligence, his ignorance, his looks. Gabriella describes a childhood in which she and her sister were often hanging around in their pyjamas, waiting for mothers of other children to invite them to their homes. Her mother would lie in bed night and day, suffering from strong migraines, refusing to communicate. When she'd finally get up, she would burst out in a fury at her daughters because of the dirt and neglect. Gabriella remembers her mother throwing all their toys, bed sheets and blankets from the veranda into the muddy backyard by way of punishing them for not arranging their room. In other cases she remembers her mother locking them in the dark storeroom for long hours, or alternatively locking herself in that same storeroom whenever they disobeyed her, until they would beg her to come out. But the neglect and the violence were nothing in comparison to the maternal invasiveness. "I can read all your thoughts", her mother would tell her, "even when I am in bed". Or: "If you think badly of me without telling me, I'll see your thoughts written on your forehead". For many years, Gabriella actually believed that her thoughts were written on her forehead and she remembers herself trying to think in English (of which her mother had a weaker command) in order to make whatever appeared on her forehead illegible. She remembers a traumatic event when her mother felt that Gabriella was keeping a secret from her. The secret had to do with the father's unfaithfulness. Gabriella ran into him while he was with his lover but did not tell anyone about it. The mother, having sharp and violent senses, felt that the child was keeping a secret from her. Gabriella remembers the mother hanging her upside down from the veranda banister and threatening to drop her if she did not confess what she (the mother) saw "written on her forehead" anyway. When Gabriella finally told her, the mother dragged her in and hit her. She remembers how trapped she felt: if she did not tell, her mother would make her fall; if she did, she would be beaten. But beyond that, she remembers throughout her childhood the feeling that she could not hide anything from her mother; that she had nowhere to run away, not even inside herself. She describes these memories mechanically, with neither emotion nor resonance.

She finished high-school, completed her compulsory army service, filled the university registration forms without being able to explain why she chose one thing rather than another. Her choices carried no meaning for her. She knew nothing about them. When I tried to search for meaning she stared at me as if she were listening to a story that was not hers. I never saw tears in her eyes, I never saw her angry, I never felt that she was in distress. Her distress was deposited in me. So was her detachment. For unbearably long sessions, I found myself listening to her without understanding what she was saying, without being able to remember the merest detail. I often caught myself day dreaming as she talked, unable to reconstruct or repeat anything she was saying. Her verbalisation was peculiar: eloquent but barely coherent, as if it lacked basic "worldly orders": a link between past and future, a plausible connection between cause and effect. She seemed to be speaking properly, but listening to her was very difficult and demanded a great effort. Whenever she got up from the couch in the end of a session, as well as at the beginning of every session at the front door (she used to come four times a week), she stared at me as if I were a complete stranger. I understood that I, too, couldn't be maintained within her as a continuous figure.

I noticed that from time to time she spoke of herself in the second-person and then shifted to the third, without being aware of these shifts. For example, during a session in which she told me about a meaningless sexual encounter she had the night before, she said: "I told myself: Gabriella, why are *you* doing this? And then I realised that *she* was doing it because *she* had nothing better to do". In this case, as in many others, the shift to the third-person went almost unmarked. When she did use the first-person, the "I", she tended to lose her grip on the plot. In other words: in her bizarre syntax, what held the story together was the third-person, but when she used it she tended to lose the experience, and so the third-person remained sterile and meaningless. On the other hand, when she used the first-person she tended to lose the story: something dissolved, spread, evacuated. She often said: "I don't remember why I started saying that or what I was trying to say. It doesn't matter anyway, I could have said anything else and it wouldn't make any difference".

This is the core of the absent inner witness: anything could testify to her, and simultaneously, nothing whatsoever testified to her. She was the thing and its opposite, the affirmation and its negation. I was aware of this because it was so unusually difficult for me to imagine her life, to hold her within me as a continuum, as a whole person. I often found myself searching for causal connections, using her past in order to endow her present with meaning, but everything dissolved. Every time a session ended I felt that she vanished. I didn't think of her until the next session. I didn't really remember her until then. She moved miles away from me, sometimes within a single day.

One morning, after two such years, she called me at the hour when our session should have taken place, mumbling something about crashing into a post in the street and losing consciousness. She told me she didn't know where she was. I actually felt it wasn't that she didn't know where she was, but that she didn't know who she was. When she finally arrived she told me that what was so difficult for her on regaining consciousness (passers by took care of her and gave her water) was that she understood that she had never been conscious. That there was no difference: "I opened my eyes because they poured water over me and they responded with cries of relief as if *she* [the transition to third-person went unnoticed, again] had come back to them, but she understood that she hadn't come back at all, that she was in the same condition she had always been". In other words, there was no difference between losing and gaining consciousness, between the "nothing that is not there" and "the nothing that is", as the poet Wallace Stevens once wrote. There was no one to wake up, no one to return.

The following night she dreamt a first dream which she brought to analysis. In the dream she was a baby with a huge head, open eyes and a speaking mouth, but instead of a whole body she had "a small scrap of a body". She couldn't move because her body was too small to hold her head, so she had to roll herself from one place to another, with the head pulling the body along instead of the other way round. At a certain point a little girl with a familiar face stands in front of her. Gabriella asks her to bring her a glass of water. The girl responds softly: "But how can you drink without a body?" And when she utters these words, Gabriella feels that her "scrap of body" sprouts a new part. So she asks the girl to repeat the words. The girl says softly: "You cannot drink without a body". Then Gabriella's body sprouts another part. The more the little girl speaks the more body Gabriella generates, until her body is almost whole. She is afraid that the girl will disappear before her body has fully evolved, and then she wakes up.

I am thinking now of the difference between the penetrating, annihilating, ever-seeing gaze of the mother, and the soft gaze of the girl in the dream on her "broken", "unfinished" parts. The mother saw through her. The girl in the dream bore witness to her. The gaze of the mother annihilated her mind as a discrete thinking space from which thoughts of her own could emanate. To a large extent, her speech was a way of not thinking, since thinking might have risked her exposure. Thinking was a dissimulation of the thought that was not allowed to be thought. It was not by accident that as a child Gabriella had tried to think in a language that was not her mother tongue. Facing both primary and unbearable secondary violence, and without the presence of a Third to suggest the possibility of transcending helplessness and gaining a vantage point—Gabriella was left trapped without a sense of validity or of singularity, without the ability to distinguish between inside and outside, between what was hers and what was not hers. Indeed, what appeared in the dream was a powerful illustration of what I called "false equality": the head bears the body rather than the body bearing the head; the testimony generates what it testifies to instead of bearing witness to what generated it. In the dream Gabriella returned from her mother-tongue to a "child-tongue" in which a non-annihilating testimony is enabled. Regaining this child-tongue restored her capacity to grow. In that sense, the act of testimony restored not only her physical body, but also the capacity to speak in the first-person, to be a speaking "I". If earlier on there was, paradoxically, "speech without body" (a speaking head with a small scrap of a body[4])—she now owned a first-person, a speaking body, a body to which speech testified and through which it could break through.

Discussion

Traumatic materials activate a process of self-annihilation. Their acidity creates a psychic hole which absorbs both the unbearable contents as well as the subject who contains them, leaving this subject imprisoned within a territory of a "negative possession", a territory in which materials are neither digested nor worked through. In traumatisation, like in trauma, there are no real survivors. There are those who do not survive, the dead, and those who seemingly survive: the "living-dead". Within the category of the living-dead there are those who are both dead and alive, as against those who are neither dead nor alive. The inner witness is what distinguishes between the living-dead and the "neither dead nor alive". The difference between a person who can testify to his or her trauma and a person who cannot testify to it, is that the one who bears witness to him or herself can transform trauma into a kind of psychic possession, whereas for the one who cannot bear witness, trauma becomes an impoverishing, reductive, and sterilising mechanism; a possession that annihilates the possessor. Lacking the function of the inner witness, Gabriella existed on a psychic plain where the conscious and the unconscious were indistinguishable. In this sense she exemplified those who are neither alive nor dead, toeing a thin line which cannot turn into a living space and does not enable a meaningful life.

Since her testimonial narrative was predominantly in the third, psychotic mode (with minor shifts to the second, metonymic mode), the main struggle within the counter-transference was the struggle to preserve myself as an experiencing and thinking subject. Gabriella's lack of coherence not only constituted an attack on her ability to link or on the linkage between us, but was also projected into me, producing a violent though terribly silent attack on my capacity to maintain a continuum of thought. The main analytic effort was, thus, the effort of preserving a space which would allow me to witness her non-thinking without turning it to an attack on my own ability to think.

The analytic work with cumulative traumatisation that turned into a "negative possession" involves a work of digestion of "empty materials" by the analyst, namely the transmission of the annihilating contents through the analyst's psychic metabolic system in order to create him or her as a witness to the patient's zones of non-digestion. The preliminary analytic work does not concern the traumatic contents themselves, but rather the metabolic mechanism that is activated by them, a mechanism that annihilates the mere possibility to join those contents as a form of memory or thought. In the course of analysis a repetitive effort to annihilate the analyst as a possible witness takes place—an effort that only a stable and stubborn analytic confrontation may succeed to work through.

Where the function of the witness is absent, nothingness isn't the absence of something, but a sort of a presence. In order to grasp the "nothing that is", as Stevens wrote, one has to agree to be the "nothing that isn't". Through this mutual metabolic process in which I found myself struggling for Gabriella's story but also evacuated with it; through the labyrinth that forced me to question the validity of my own perceptions and understanding; through my vanishing point in which I lost not only her, at the end of every session, but also myself—the moment in which I found her was made possible.

Guests with no hosts, presences with no name: a discussion of Waiting for Godot

Samuel Beckett's enigmatic play *Waiting for Godot* (1953) places its two protagonists as well as their repetitive discourse in a spaceless and time-less universe, as an illustration to the human existence he perceived as both meaningless and absurd. The play not only confronts the very experience of existing in no-space and no-time, but also stretches it up to its tragic and comic edges. Though Beckett's overt intention was not to describe the inner world of specific characters but to sketch human existence in general—the dialogue that takes place between them reflects in an extremely accurate manner the features of what I called "a psychotic testimonial narrative". My discussion, therefore, will try to explore the syntax rules that are compelled on the emotional discourse, both intra-psychically and inter-psychically, by the absence of the inner witness.

One of the clearest and most vivid illustrations of the absent inner witness is the two protagonists' (Vladimir and Estragon) complete inability to testify to themselves, to their biography, to any sequence (Estragon: "What did we do yesterday?" Vladimir: "What did we do yesterday?" p. 14), to their disorientation in space and time ("But what Saturday? And is it Saturday? Is it not rather Sunday? Or Monday? Or Friday?" p. 15), or their inability to identify anything as even famil-iar (Estragon: "In my opinion we were here". Vladimir: "You recognise the place?" Estragon: "I didn't say that." p. 14). This illustrates what I described above as the absence of any hierarchy or individuation as well as a complete fusion of inside and outside, and of cause and effect. Remembering the past—much as imagining the future—is linked to the capacity of transcending the present; without the capacity to tran-scend the concrete present, whether onward, backward or inward, self experience is one of a psychic void, a space that has no limits and therefore does not demand or enable satiation.

At a certain point in the play another couple appears: Pozzo, Lucky's master, treats him as half-slave half-beast of burden. This makes it very difficult for both Vladimir and Estragon (and for the readers) to hold on to the knowledge that Lucky is actually a human being. Although his actions make it very clear that Lucky is not a beast—Pozzo's attitude towards him turns him into one, and it seems easier for us to adjust to this contradiction than to keep him in our minds as human. This is the enormous power of testimony: Pozzo testifies to Lucky as a beast and thereby turns him into one. Vladimir and Estragon, whose leverage on both themselves and the other is lacking, cannot but collude with this bestialisation. Their alienation, their lack of both inner and outer context, their inability to create a narrative—turn them into witnesses to everything and to nothing, into non-judgmental witnesses to whatever they encounter. Being characters within a story that lacks a narrator, they are unable to take an ethical, historical or emotional stance towards what they see, and they certainly are not capable of exceeding it into a truly symbolic vantage point. Within their discourse everything is true and nothing is truthful.

Pozzo tells Vladimir and Estragon that relations of any kind might be reversed at any moment. Then he explains to them that the amount of tears in the world is constant: each time someone starts crying someone else stops. This applies also to laughter (ibid. p. 32). The affirmation that tears and laughter constitute a constant reservoir and each time someone takes a quantity for him or herself another lacks it, neutralises the personal meaning of emotional expression. Lucky stops crying not because something or someone calmed him down, but simply because Estragon started to cry. In this sense, Lucky's tears and Pozzo's cruelty testify to neither of them. This is what makes the situation eminently reversible: no one has any claim or hold on anything. And since the self is fundamentally constituted through possession, being an assembling structure that marks certain materials as "me materials" and others as "not-me materials"—the inability to differentiate between them abolishes the sense of a singular self. Thus, the subject turns from being the sum total of his or her own parts into an accidental and an ever-changing sample of characteristics. Where there is no self one can testify to, there is no other either, and surely there are no relations with such an-other. If any relations can be reversed at any moment, as Pozzo said, there is no psychic reality that can be accumulated as a memory, as a thought or as a matrix of mind on the basis of which future or past events can be predicted and understood.

Later on, Pozzo orders Lucky to think, telling the others that Lucky cannot think without his hat (ibid. p. 41). Two elements seem critical here: first of all, the order "think!" contradicts thinking. And indeed, Lucky's text (resembling, in a way, Gabriella's text) is coherent but completely senseless. Rather than testifying to him as a thinking subject, his "thinking" abolishes him as one. Psychotic thinking or psychotic syntax is actually a way to preserve thinking through non-thinking. If we relate to Pozzo and Lucky as a "primary thinking couple" (since they maintain a kind of symbiosis in a world with no significant others), we understand that Pozzo's violent appropriation of Lucky's "space of thinking" annihilates Lucky as a subject. In this sense Lucky's only way to preserve a discrete thinking space is by not thinking.

Why can't Lucky think without his hat? There is a total inversion and fusion of the primary conditions of cause and effect: The hat, here, is the condition for the existence and functioning of the head (so that to stop him from thinking they remove Lucky's hat, not his head), instead of the head being the prior condition for the hat. A similar inversion occurs between Lucky and his tasks: when he falls to the ground what helps him regain stability is the basket that is put in his hand. His task defines him instead of being defined by him: the basket holds him instead of being held by him. This is the relation of "false equality".

"And then nobody ever recognises us", says Vladimir to Estragon while they are trying to understand whether Pozzo and Lucky are complete strangers or unrecognised acquaintances (ibid. p. 48). The inability to assimilate the new to the familiar is characteristic of the experience of the absent inner witness. The subject's ability to bear witness to him or herself is always based on a permanent vantage point and on the assumption that the self, though subject to change, is also constant. An absent inner witness turns existence into an ever-becoming, thus does not enable the establishment of a continuous self (Amir, 2008). When a boy enters the scene in order to inform Vladimir and Estragon that Godot will not be arriving today either, Vladimir addresses him: "Tell him you saw us". And after a pause: "You did see us, didn't you?" (ibid. p. 51).

An absent inner witness leads to the subject's desperate, existential dependence on the testimony of the other. But this testimony depends upon the subject's ability to preserve it. This is the psychotic paradox: since the psychotic subject lacks experience of a constant self—she or he depends on the other as a constant witness. Tragically, they cannot possibly make use of that other as a constant witness as long as they are unable to preserve any constant witnesses within themselves.

The last episode in *Waiting for Godot* which I wish to highlight is the renewed and final encounter between the two couples, Estragon/Vladimir and Pozzo/Lucky. Pozzo is now blind and Lucky is dumb. Vladimir forces Pozzo to bear witness, namely insists on asking him when was it that he became blind and Lucky turned dumb. Pozzo becomes furious:

> Have you not done tormenting me with your accursed time? It's abominable. When! When! One day, is that not enough for you, one day like any other day, one day he went dumb, one day I went blind, one day we'll go deaf, one day we were born, one day we'll die, the same day, the same second, is that not enough for you? (Ibid. p. 89)

Pozzo holds on to the refusal to be the owner of his own dream, of his own fate, of his own history. For him each moment contains everything and nothing, since the "I" that owns the moment is absent from it. Vladimir asks:

> Am I sleeping now? Tomorrow, when I wake, or think I do, what shall I say of today? [...] At me too someone is looking, of me too someone is saying, He is sleeping, he knows nothing, let him sleep on. (Ibid. pp. 90–91)

The confusion between sleep and wakefulness touches not only the inability to be "the dreamer who understands the dream" or "the dreamer who makes the dream understandable" (Grotstein, 2000), but also the inability to be the dreamer who *dreams* the dream. A person who does not dream, as Ogden (2003) says, can neither wake up nor fall asleep. Indeed, the protagonists of *Waiting for Godot* are neither awake nor asleep, and as such they move about in a dream without a dreamer, or an undreamable dream, which due to their refusal to own it leaves them outside their own selves: guests with no hosts, presences with no name.

Nausea as the refusal of a mother-tongue: the psychosomatic, metaphoric, metonymic, and psychotic expression*

The drama that takes place on the bodily stage is always of an exceptional intensity. Not only does the body frequently place us on the seam between existence and non-existence, but its syntax is very hard to interpret or to resist. One reason why somatic symptoms tend to be especially persistent is related to the fact that the symptom animates the body. Often, behind spectacular and colourful somatic drama hides a sense of death and emptiness. The dramatic symptom enlivens the body and the psyche, as well as the texture of object relations.

From its earliest days, psychoanalysis has addressed the role of the body in the development of psychic functioning. Freud (1895d), in his early research on hysteria, did not distinguish the physiological from the psychological in terms of their importance. In his three essays on infantile sexuality (1905d) he used psychology in order to shed light on the biology of human sexuality by following the multiple transformations of sexual energy within the body. The *Project for a Scientific Psychology* (1950a) constitutes his attempt to render phenomena he

---

*This chapter is based on a paper that won the 2013 IPA Sacerdoti Prize.

encountered in his research on hysteria in terms of energies. The ego in this text is a somatic-psychic ego which functions on the physiological level as a collection of neurons constantly recharged with energy, and on the psychological level as an agent whose objective is to achieve the dominance of the reality principle and secondary processes. The notion that the ego, before anything else, is a bodily ego, the product of bodily senses as a whole—and those linked with the surfaces of the body more specifically—appears later in *The Ego and the Id* (1923b). Ferenzci (1932) argued that the human individual has two memory systems: while the subjective memory system includes feelings and bodily sensations, the objective memory system includes external events and sensations ascribed to one's surroundings. The earlier an event, the more likely it is to have been encoded in the subjective memory, that is, as a bodily sensation or response. Having been inscribed in the body, certain types of memory can only re-surface in the body. Ferenczi considered the occurrence of bodily symptoms in the course of psychotherapy as evidence of the return of these type of memories—a return made possible because and as part of the process of therapeutic regression. Wilhelm Reich (1949) was interested in the characteristic way the body is held, and subsequently in the body's blockages to full libidinal release. Melanie Klein (1923, 1952) perceived the body as the first site of psychic activity. For each psychic mechanism there exists a somatic archetype and each bodily sensation is represented by an emotional attitude vis-à-vis the mother. The mechanisms of introjection and projection are thus based on the physical mechanisms of ingesting and expelling. Anger and negative feelings hark back to the physical mechanism of the production and excretion of faeces; love is based on sensations of fullness and satiety. The Kleinian infant's body is construed as a site of tempestuous psychic activity and bodily functions are perceived as types of infantile relations to the world as well as to itself (Durban, 2002). Winnicott, too, regarded bodily experience as the substrate of psychic formation. In his article "Mind and its relation to psyche-soma" (1949) he described the developing individual as a mode of being within which psyche and soma are inextricable and become distinct only as a function of the observer's viewpoint. In fact, the meaning of the word "psyche" is the imaginary processing of physical-somatic experience. Gila Horesh (2006) mentions Winnicott's article "Ego distortions in terms of true and false self" (1960a), in which he describes the stage by which the patient allows contact, however partial, with hitherto inaccessible regions associated with his or her true self. It happens often that the patient falls ill in the course of this process, thereby giving the therapist the opportunity to assume the role previously taken by the false self. Taking up Winnicott's observation, Horesh suggests considering physical illness as an occasion for introspection and for a different type of encounter between patient and therapist.

Esther Bick, in her article "The experience of the skin in early object relations" (1968), defined the phenomenon of "the second skin": In the most primitive stage of infantile development, the various parts of personality are felt to exist without any unifying or connecting force of their own. Thus they are held passively, with the skin serving as a connecting envelope. Not only do the parts of the body require a skin envelope in order to be contained as a whole, the parts of the personality, too, are experienced as dispersed and in need of a skin-like envelope within which they can be contained. This internal function of the containment of self parts depends on the internalisation of an external object, experienced as capable of fulfilling this function on behalf of the infant, in the very first stages of life, and the assumption is that if such an object (serving as a skin-container) is available—then the function it fulfils will be internalised. In the absence of this experience the infant is left with a sense of non-containment, and in order not to suffer the threat of disintegration evolves an artificial envelope which is felt as though it holds together the inner parts. Such a second skin can reveal itself in a variety of forms: muscle rigidity, gestural rituals, clinging to certain types of clothing, intellectual obsessiveness—all these are "second skins". Sticking to a rigorous routine or choosing difficult tasks may also supply the fragile self with a sense of an outline (Bick, 1986, 1968). Didier Anzieu (1989) believes the skin has both a sealing as well as a communicating function. In addition to demarcating the psychic body, the skin is the surface on which communication first occurs as it is there that the first rhythms are recorded and given various qualities of texture and touch. Beyond sealing and communicating, the skin also serves to connect between outside and inside, between other and self. It is, in fact, the primary zone of distinction between the experience of "me" and the experience of "not-me". Ogden's "autistic-contiguous position" (1989a) further extends these notions. In the autistic-contiguous position sensory experiences—mainly located on the surface of the skin—are the sole means of generating psychological meaning and thus constituting the groundwork of self experience. Each time it rests its cheek on the mother's breast the infant receives a sense of form. Breastfeeding gives it a sense of rhythm and continuity. As its gums forcefully enclose the mother's nipple the infant derives a sense of edge or boundary. Thus, the autistic-contiguous experience has a rhythmic quality which transforms into an experience of ongoingness, a quality of demarcation that becomes an experience of place, and qualities of hardness, cold, warmth, and texture that make for the initial outline of "who I am".

Frances Tustin (1981, 1986, 1990) argued that when bodily separateness is experienced as traumatic, the infant experiences the space between bodies as full of horrifying and destructive annihilating substances. The reaction to such danger is what Tustin called "endogenous auto-sensuousness". Her notion of "auto-sensuous reactions" refers to the various self-stimulating and self-soothing behaviours that are typical of autistic children. Two of these behavioural patterns are "autistic sensation objects" (1980) and "autistic sensation shapes" (1984), which are two types of reaction that serve to enfold the child in a protective sensory shell. This defence, generated by the infant itself, includes autistic sensation objects which allow the child to feel strong and safe, as well as autistic sensation shapes which soothe and pacify.

In his book *From the Eclipse of the Body to the Dawn of Thought* (2004) Ferrari introduces the notion of the "concrete original object", referring to a primordial consciousness of what is later called "the body". This is a global sense of "existing in space" as a collection of body sensations which while not represented in the mind constitutes the very grounding of mentalization. This is, in fact, the very first object to which the infant relates. Ferrari assumes the parallel development of two early relational modes: the relationship between self and body, and the relationship between self and object. These two modes of relating interweave tightly and dynamically and cannot, in fact, be prised apart. It is in the course of development, and through the mother's work of reverie, that the volume of sensory phenomena gradually shrinks, making space for mental inscriptions which cast "a shadow" on the original concrete object. This process of damping, which needless to say is never fully exhausted, is necessary considering the flooding that chaotic bodily sensations cause. Michal Reick (2011) draws attention, in this context, to bodily sensations that are not represented in the patient's mind, thus existing in the form of "body memory" outside the ego's integration. Such bodily sensations enfold the memory of an impinging environment which caused cumulative traumatisation. Since the conditions allowing psychic integration of the traumatic occurrence have failed to emerge, there is no way to recollect it. Reick discusses states when, as opposed to remembering through the body (Mitrani, 1995), the patient "transfers" the memory to the analyst's body in the course of the analysis.[1]

Psychosomatic drama is often linked with primary trauma and huge difficulty concerning separation and separateness. Difficulty in transforming body into language—or the raw primary data of experience into words and symbols—situates the psychosomatic drama at an extremely early stage of development prior to mentalization. When the mother-infant relation is dysfunctional, the infant finds it hard to internalise the maternal object enough to dare losing and recreating it as a symbol, thus form a representation of its absence (Kristeva, 1987a; Green, 1988). In such cases the infant goes on generating physical symptoms as a way of keeping the mother close as well as expressing his inability to mourn her in the process of internalisation (Amir, 2008).

There is nevertheless a certain degree of symbolic hierarchy even in this flow of somatic phenomena. Different levels of symbolisation can be identified within psychosomatic language, ranging from psychosomatic expressions that are a live, concrete metaphor for the repressed contents, all the way to those psychosomatic expressions that arise as a reaction to traumatic experience in a manner whose meaning is extremely difficult to catch. In this regard, MacDougall (1989) argued that where experiences are not successfully repressed, thus gaining no internal representation, they cannot even serve to generate neurotic symptoms. When, temporarily or for a longer stretch of time, the psyche is unable to restore what has been expelled from consciousness in the form of symptoms, the release of dreams, or any other type of mental activity, it enters a state of deprivation. It is likely, in such a case, that the psyche will respond by somatisation. Like in early pre-linguistic childhood the somatically reacting psyche will directly access the "thing"—not the word that would represent it. The bodily reaction is a primitive representation of the experience—but one that cannot turn it into a meaningful experience or enable release. MacDougall mentions in this context a phenomenon she calls "archaic hysteria". Unlike its neurotic counterpart, which is a more developed form mainly related to anxiety associated with sexual satisfaction and desires—archaic hysteria concerns the very desire or right to exist. These are not anxieties of the more "developed" kind, but ones that occur where personal identity or life itself are under a threat of extinction. These states are marked by damage to a body part or bodily function without organic reason. MacDougall identified one very particular dysfunction where the body's behaviour resembles the biological reaction to danger by seeming to want to get rid of toxic materials (excrement), or by seeming to try and hold on to something (air) which threatens to empty out. These bodily manifestations come in reaction to messages from the psyche, which is using them to try and cope with experiences it perceives as a threat. These bodily phenomena, which are actually life-endangering at times, have a psychological meaning—but one of a pre-symbolic kind. Since the anxieties involved are unavailable to symbolic, reflective, verbal representation—no neurotic symptoms evolve. What remains is the thing itself, without any possibility of distancing.

Metaphoric, metonymic, and psychotic psychosomatic expressions

In "A question prior to any possible treatment of psychosis" (1958) Lacan writes about the notion of "forclusion" in the context of psychosis. Repression and forclusion differ in that while the first aims to remove a thought or an image from consciousness, the latter removes it from the unconscious. In other words, while forclusion casts the materials out of the unconscious, repression strives to fix them there. While repression is part of normal psychic functioning—though under certain conditions it has neurotic outcomes that impair functioning—forclusion consists of a violent rejection of psychic reality and its implications are catastrophic. It leads to psychosis rather than neurosis.

Following Lacan's ideas, and continuing the previous chapter's discussion of testimonial narratives, I would like to propose a distinction between three types of psychosomatic expression located on the continuum between neurosis and psychosis: the metaphoric, the metonymic and the psychotic expressions.

What is the difference between metaphor and metonymy and how does psychotic expression elude the continuity between the former two? Metaphor and metonymy are two forms of semantic shift, that is, two modes of transition from one semantic field to another. Metaphor is the use of a word or expression in a borrowed rather than simple sense, or rather the use of the characteristics of one concept to illuminate another. Metaphor is based on analogy, namely on a relationship of similarity between two semantic fields. The sentence "My love is a rose" does not imply that the rose itself is the beloved one but that something in the beloved one's features resembles those of a rose.

Metonymy, by contrast, is a figurative tool that illustrates something by replacing it with another that is situated close to it in time or space, or that belongs in the same context. The result is not logical in the simple sense, thus can only be understood through the proximity between the two elements. This is how the expression "the White House" comes to stand for the notion of "the President's spokesperson". As opposed to metaphor, in metonymy there is no transfer of characteristics between the two elements (the President's spokesperson is not meant to share features with the White House). The connection between them is associative only in a way that allows us to perceive the one as representative of the other.

In his article "Two aspects of language and two types of linguistic disturbances" (1956), Roman Jakobson presents metaphor and metonymy as polar opposites rather than parts of the hierarchical order in which they are more commonly seen. He stresses the similarity that metaphor installs between its signifiers *vs.* the contiguity typical of metonymy. Each of these modes of transposition, he argues, relies on different cognitive skills. While metaphor is based on the cognitive ability to convert, metonymy implies the cognitive ability to connect and contextualise, namely the ability to create continuity and to identify something as part of, and following from, a context. Jakobson divides the aphasic patients with whom his article is concerned into those who suffer from impaired identification of similarities as opposed to patients whose ability to combine and contextualise is affected. Lacan's distinction between metaphor and metonymy diverges from Jakobson's. Though, following the latter, he associates metaphor with the axis of linguistic selection and metonymy with that of combination, metaphor for him acts to constitute meaning while metonymy resists meaning: the metonymic drive is related to the desire to recover the lost Real. Metaphor, by contrast, is associated with the symptom whose creation is a constructive process in which new meaning is created.

Bar-On, in her article "It cuts both ways: an analysis of the psychological discourse on self injury from a linguistic point of view" (in press) dedicated to the phenomenon of self-injury, discusses the differences between metaphorical and metonymical models of interpretation. She quotes Bollas (1993) who describes a self-injuring patient who compares the cut she has inflicted on herself and the resulting bleeding with her vagina and menstruation. The patient's act of self-injury is framed by means of a metaphoric formulation (in which the cut symbolizes her sexual organ), but Bar-On sees it as a metonymic one, emphasizing the continuum of cut, anticipation and bleeding. Thus, In contrast with the metaphorical formulation typical to classic psychoanalytic theory, Bar-On suggests a metonymic model of interpretation of the symptom of self-injury. In this model, self-injury is not seen as symbolising repressed contents but as part of a continuum emerging between pain and treatment, between cut and soothing, between being injured and receiving care. Bar-On claims that the only metonymic description of the act of self injury is offered by the anti-dissociative model (Bromberg, 1998) which conceives of self-injury as a way of escaping survival-oriented dissociative experience by means of the shock caused by pain and the sight of blood. Self-injury, here, is presented as a way of reanimating the metonymic skills of combination and contextualisation, which are damaged during the dissociative process—a plea to create continuity within the dissociation, which is characterised by lapses in continuity, interruptions and disengagements. Bar-On's therapeutic experience shows that the self-cutting method is an extremely calculated one, in which the array of cuts forms a kind of map on which one route leads to another. The new cut is perceived in terms of its metonymic continuity and its significance is based on its relationship with the previous cuts. Thus, self-injurers may be understood as suffering from an impairment of the metonymic axis reflected in an inability to maintain a continuous experience of existence, as well as in the creation of rigid and destructive rituals as a result (Bar-On, in press).

A significant difference between a metaphoric and a metonymic use of the body can also be assumed to exist in the involuntary psychosomatic phenomena—not just in self-initiated bodily acts. Within the extensive domain of psychosomatic phenomena, symbolic somatic phenomena—those which while resisting consciousness nevertheless participate in the symbolic order—can be considered metaphorical. The metaphoric psychosomatic expressions are estranged formulations, in a "foreign language" and using a different conceptual system, of something a person either cannot, or is not willing to, fully recognize. In essence, these phenomena resemble the conversion phenomena typical of neurotic hysteria.

The more primitive somatic phenomena may be seen as metonymic phenomena. Here there is no rich expression—not even in a different language—of repressed material, but a limited shift from the psychic scene to that of the body, or from one physical scene to another physical one. It is a shift whose symbolicity is hard to trace back, and which is more reminiscent of what MacDougall called "archaic hysteria" (MacDougall, 1989).

In addition to metaphoric expression (which symbolises the traumatic memory) and metonymic expression (which maintains an experiential line with the traumatic memory without symbolising or representing it), there exists a third type of psychosomatic expression which I would like to point out. This is a physical phenomenon which on the one hand is inaccessible to interpretation, while on the other does not reanimate the traumatic experience. It is marked by constituting an attack on any attempt at representation as such, resisting any type of linkage. It is anchored in the body not because the body is the scene of traumatic memory but because it is the scene prior to the split constituted by language. Unlike metonymic expression which entails both a reminder of the traumatic and the attempt to overcome it (for example, by forging an experience of continuity within the dissociative disconnection)—psychotic psychosomatic expression not only does not hold meaning (as its metaphoric counterpart does), or maintain continuity (as does the metonymic)—but actually attacks subjectivity in a manner that makes any formation of an "experiencing I" impossible. This expression preserves a gratifying and magical union with the primary object without the barrier of words.

Lacan discusses the formation of subjectivity as being based on an experience of lack. The subject is constituted at the point in time when he or she enters the "Symbolic order", through the mother's interpretation of the Real. Side by side with the experience itself, the infant is given an interpretation that renders the experience meaningful. This interpretation introduces raw experience into the order of language. The intersection between these experiences, that gain an identical category, is what the child experiences as that category: pain, tickling, cold, missing. There is however always a remainder or surplus that stays outside this intersection. This surplus, lost in the process of symbolisation, stays outside the order of language and becomes the object of desire (object a).[2] Psychic motion is always directed towards that object of desire—and it is through this motion that the subject is constituted qua living subject. In contrast to the concept of the object as satisfying—Lacan introduces the lack of the object as constitutive to the creation of the subject in the first place. No psychic motion will be possible without the experience of lack. Analysis, according to his view, can be seen as the process that comes to identify the specific metaphor through which the subject represents the wholeness for which he or she yearns. The identification of this metaphor never aims to fulfil the desire but comes to reveal its specific expressions which are what makes up the singular subject. What characterises a person is the mode in which his or her desire asserts itself and the ways in which it finds pleasure. Lacan calls the illusion of appeasing lack "phantasm". This is the collective name for all the privately held myths of wholeness which together create the subject's singularity.

Psychotic psychosomatic expression is an expression which creates, through the consummate chaos of bodily experience, an illusion of union without lack. One of its hallmarks is the huge satisfaction it offers in its wake. This is pure *"jouissance"* (pleasure); one that is associated with the incestuous union with the mother and with one's lingering in the Real—prior to being introduced to the order of language.

Over the years, I treated three female patients who each reported an unexplained phenomenon of nausea. Differences in their experience of nausea helped me to identify, within the seemingly identical concrete physical complaint, significant variations in the levels of symbolisation. The first of these patients was the daughter of an unstable shifty mother who made frequent manipulative use of her child's physical and emotional needs in order to subjugate her. From as long as she can recall, this patient remembers her own reaction to any response to her needs (including when her needs were met in analysis) as one of physical nausea ("I hate it when you listen to me. It makes me sick"). For this patient nausea represented the emotional rejection she felt towards all forms of maternal nourishment. Her unconscious use of nausea was a metaphoric one: rejection and nausea share some features and their relationship is analogous: even if the one is located in the psyche and the other in the body, both are forms of distancing.

My second patient reported feeling a rising nausea each time she thought she wished to be pregnant. The picture, here, was more complicated. Like in the case of the first patient her nausea could have been perceived as a metaphoric expression if it had stood for her unconscious attempt to remove the whole issue of pregnancy. But here nausea occurred as though it marked pregnancy itself. In the course of therapy intense memories emerged of a severe nausea her mother suffered from during her pregnancy with the patient's younger sister who was born with cerebral palsy. The nausea phenomenon, in this case, can be viewed as a metonymic expression in which the connection between nausea and pregnancy is not based on an analogy (in which both are metaphoric removals of the pregnancy issue)—but is an associative connection, creating a continuum with the anxiety associated with the mother's failed pregnancy and the physically impaired sister's birth, a continuum that enabled the patient to be in touch with her violence and guilt without having to remember them. It was her way of reviving the anxiety inducing scene in her own body without having to reflect on it. In both cases, interpretation caused a significant relief.

My third patient was the only daughter of a middle aged mother. Raising her by herself, with no father, the mother forced her daughter to share her bed until the girl's late adolescence, creating both a psychological and physical symbiotic relationship with her. Trying to ensure her daughter would shun any relationship that might unsettle this symbiosis—the mother would tell her hair-raising tales about men, especially about her biological father. The patient grew up with the feeling that any distance she would take from her mother and her worldview would mean death. The two did not communicate through words but used body gestures and sounds which, like a private and secret language, were only partially intelligible to outsiders. The patient, whose verbal ability was extremely poor and inexpressive, said she suffered a chronic sense of nausea. She did not describe it as something that came and went, in response, for instance, to certain smells or actions. Nor did she report on a particular sense of distress in relation to her nausea. The nausea was simply there, chronic and indistinct, lacking in outline or associations, meaningless and resisting meaning. It existed, both in my patient's psyche as well as in the therapeutic sessions, like standing air with no movement, something one does not notice yet without which nothing else can be noticed. Nausea, here, enacted an attack on any type of linking, a shackling to the traumatic Real which tells no story and wants to hear no story. This was a psychotic psychosomatic expression: an expression belonging to the class of somatic phenomena that are not physical representations of a memory but rather an attack on representation. This was not a flight from the trauma but a welding with it. It

was a meaning-denying process that came to being through the attempt
to hold on to the Real and be held by it.

These illustrations show an identical physical phenomenon in three
different levels of symbolisation and in three different patients. But often
(and in that sense the approach I am proposing differs from Lacan's)
what we encounter is a mixed psychosomatic phenomena in which shifts
between the three levels of symbolisation can be traced within what on
the face of it appears as one obstinate psychosomatic spectacle.

Nausea as a refusal of a mother-tongue

What, actually, is nausea? It is an experience which simultaneously
expresses fusion and distancing. We tend to feel nauseous when there is
insufficient distance between us and something or someone, that is, in
response to experiencing it, whether consciously or not, as too close. The
thing itself does not necessarily arouse objective repulsion. It may be an
intense smell of perfume that pierces our nostrils, a face that pushes
itself too close to ours, an imagined contact with something we usually
avoid. Repulsion is bound up with the collapse of distance: it comes to
"repair" or restore that distance by vomiting out the intrusive object.
Nausea, then, is both the result of the loss of distance, as well as what
rehabilitates it. It is an expression of too much closeness which generates, or imposes, removal. In this sense nausea belongs in the domain
of coping with separation and separateness. The lack of distance from
the object—any object—seems to resonate with the absence of primary
distance from the maternal body and the exaggerated proximity to its
smells, secretions, and intimacy. This is the excess proximity which Julia
Kristeva called "the abject" (1982). Nausea, it could be argued, signals
an original incestuous desire—even when it is associated with inanimate objects, smells, types of food, or sights that bear no direct relation
to the mother herself.

I already mentioned Piera Aulagnier (2001) who wrote copiously
about the young mother's incestuous desire for her own mother, a desire
that actually constitutes a death wish vis-à-vis the infant to which she
is about to give birth. Incestuous desire is always directed against life.
Unlike symbolic nausea which is a form of separation, as Kristeva
writes in her essay (1982), namely a process of self-formation by means
of repulsion, of spitting out—there is a kind of nausea, too, which
does not come to represent the wish for separateness but rather fulfils

the wish to not separate. In contrast to the symbolic psychosomatic expression—rather than constituting the subject it annihilates it by erasing the basic experience of lack, allowing neither desire nor the psychic motion resulting from it.

Somatic phenomena of this kind are far more dangerous than symbolic symptoms since they actually provide the subject with a real object in the form of pain, bleeding (see Marie Cardinal's *Les Mots Pour Le Dire*, 1984³), and nausea. This is where the somatic phenomenon transforms into an object in its own right, an object whose archaic attraction relates to its being meaningless and open to nothing but repetition. Repetition, in this case, is not repetition of the signifier but of the collapse of the signifier in the face of the signified. The psychotic somatic expression is experienced as ego-syntonic rather than ego-dystonic: it is a phenomenon that neither torments the subject—nor is it experienced as imposed on it from outside or from within. It is rather inaccessible to interpretation or does not ask for it. It may indeed not even entail a sense of distress. Essentially resisting subjectivity and the formation of an "experiencing I", psychotic somatic expressions are usually not accompanied by pain. There co-exist, in every bodily phenomenon, a symbolic as well as an a-symbolic component which interrelate with varying degrees of dominance. The symbolic component uses the body metaphorically or metonymically, and is the part that is open to interpretation. The a-symbolic component, however, uses the body in a psychotic way—which does not allow for interpretation and attacks any such possibility. The more dominant this a-symbolic component, the more dangerous is the somatic phenomenon to psychic growth.

In Jean-Paul Sartre's *Nausea*, the protagonist ([1938] 2007), Antoine Roquentin, tries to make sense of the nausea he feels increasingly whenever he comes into contact with people and objects. While this nausea puts a distance between him and whatever surrounds him, equally much it becomes something that he is assimilated with. While generating a sense of singularity and aloofness—his nausea also has absorbing qualities and is experienced as irrepressible and overwhelming. The nausea as it evolves in the course of this novel is very reminiscent of what Lacan describes as primary experience before it was crossed out by language. Nausea, in this sense, renders the encounter with the absence of outline that characterise what stays outside any symbolic order. As the protagonist is a historian, someone who ostensibly has the capacity to use symbolic language, the novel is a fascinating fluctuation between the symbolic state, experienced as empty and mechanical, and the state of nausea, which is a state of collapse testifying to the traumatic Real.

> [...] and from time to time, out of the corner of my eye I see a reddish flash covered with hair. It is a hand. (Ibid. p. 19)

The transition from "a reddish flash covered with hair" to "It is a hand" is the transition from the Real to the Symbolic. Nausea is linked to the "reddish flash" and comes as a reaction to it; watching a reddish flash on the skin of an arm means being intolerably close to that skin, to its blemishes, to its smells, its shades and hues. The statement: "It is a hand", in contrast, is a way to escape nausea and gain distance from the object that arouses it. This is, in fact, how the unbearable sight of the skin is caught in the filter of language for the sake of survival. It exemplifies symbolic organisation in the face of the intolerable encounter with the somatic Real.

> The Nausea is not inside me: I feel it out there in the wall, in the suspenders, everywhere around me. It makes itself one with the café. I am the one who is within it. (Ibid. pp. 19–20)

Nausea is associated with the absence of boundaries. Although the "I" may seem to separate, reject and remove by means of it—nausea actually supplies that "I" with a much greater, much more capacious "Other"[4] in which the "I" becomes absorbed and which helps it to deny the experience of lack and desire. This denial comes not only at the cost of the negation of psychic motion but also of the negation of the subject as the owner of this motion. Rather than being the one who experiences—the subject within the territory of the Real is the experience itself. He does not feel agony: he *is* agony.

> I stop suddenly: there is a flaw, I have seen a word pierce through the web of sensations. I suppose that this word will soon take the place of several images I love. I must stop quickly and think of something else. (Ibid. p. 33)

This is the crux of the existential paradox Sartre describes by means of his protagonist: The word replaces the experience. In a sense the rejection of the word is a way to fend off the death it spells, but the preservation of experience is a death sentence for the experiencing subject. Language is the attempt to thwart the extinction of the moment by inserting it into the chain of signifiers. However, language is not merely the attempt to immortalise but also what nullifies eternity.

> I have never before had such a strong feeling that I was devoid of secret dimensions, confined within the limits of my body. (Ibid. p. 33)

Non-existent as a subject, Roquentin is limited to his somatic existence solely. This is the reason why he lacks the dimension of secrecy—something that is reserved for those who use folds of consciousness and are able to reveal and to hide. Within the territory of the Real there is neither covering nor uncovering, neither proximity nor distance.

> And the IDEA is there, this great white mass which so disgusted me then [...]. It has rolled itself into a ball, it stays there like a large cat. (Ibid. p. 36)

Words and thoughts, within the domain of the Real, are identical to external objects. This is very reminiscent—and not by coincidence—of Bion's description of psychotic thinking (1956, 1959). One outcome of the psychotic individual's use of projective identification, Bion argues, is his or her inability to internalise. Unable to link between his or her objects, the psychotic individual can only compress them or pile them up. Projective identification is a psychotic alternative to the functions of repression and internalisation. Thus, in lieu of an interior experience comes an experience of concrete space into which objects can be put and from which they can be thrown out without their having undergone any transformation.

Roquentin, in his nausea state, is too close to the body of things. Due to this lack of distance he is exposed to innumerable details and finds himself repelled by this plurality. Language and words are a manner of taking a step back: they are the psyche's way of gathering the massive volume of details under one name, one title, one signifier, thus to alleviate the experience of the manifold. "It is a hand" is a statement which makes it possible not to go, time and again, through the whole mass of reddish flash. Roquentin, who rejects language and the distance it enables, remains stuck in the profusion of details. This plurality and proximity are what creates his nausea.

> I felt the afternoon all through my heavy body. Not my afternoon, but theirs, the one a hundred thousand Bouvillois were going to live in common. (Sartre, 1938, p. 50)

In the absence of any outline generated by the "experiencing I", any experience belongs and does not belong to it simultaneously. Language is not only the filter or sieve through which raw experience passes. It is also what makes possible the illusion of a specific, distinct experience— an experience which carries the stamp of the "singular I". When, however, there is no subject, no "speaking I", general or public experience is not separated from personal singular one and cannot be transformed through it.

> Thoughts are the dullest things. Duller than flash. They stretch out and there's no end to them and they leave a funny taste in the mouth. Then there are words, inside the thoughts, unfinished words, a sketchy sentence which constantly returns [...]. For example, this sort of painful rumination: I *exist*, I am the one who keeps it up. I. The body lives by itself once it has begun. But thoughts— I am the one who continues it, unrolls it [...]. If I could keep myself from thinking! (Ibid. p. 99)

For Roquentin, the thought that is situated in language, fed by it and constructed from words, is bland since it enfolds and preserves the biggest illusion of all: the illusion of existence. Through the regurgitation of words this illusion preserves the thinking subject and thereby the illusion of an existing subject. Sartre's protagonist understands something that Lacan formulated no less accurately: it is not that "I think therefore I am", but rather: where I think, there I am not[5].

> They exist running, breathing, beating, all soft, all gently breathless, leaving me breathless, he says he's breathless; existence takes my thoughts from behind and gently expands them *from behind*; someone takes me from behind, they force me to think from behind, therefore be something. (Ibid. p. 102)

Here we can follow the shift between the domain of the Real—in which the phenomenon resides as it is, un-owned ("all gently breathless")—and the Symbolic domain, where the self makes its entry ("leaving *me* breathless") and where, almost automatically, the transition to the third-person ("*he* says he's breathless") occurs. It is, then, in the shift from the Real to the Symbolic that the subject appears, but experience in its full actuality is lost. From being an experience which rather than being "of the body"—"is the body", it transforms into an experience of the first-person which, as part of the process of representation, comprises the distance of the third-person, the distance that enables both naming and reflection.

> I am in the midst of things, nameless things. Alone without words, defenceless, they surround me, are beneath me, behind me, above me. They demand nothing, they don't impose themselves: they are there. [...] I couldn't stand any more. I could no longer stand things being so close. (Ibid. pp. 125–126)

The psychotic domain enacts a traumatic combination of "nameless dread" (Bion, 1962a, 1965) with constant nausea which is connected to the fact that where no names can be given no distance can be maintained.

> The Nausea has not left me and I don't believe it will leave me so soon; but I no longer have to bear it, it is no longer an illness or a passing fit: it is I. [...] The diversity of things, their individuality, were only an appearance, a veneer. This veneer had melted, leaving soft, monstrous masses, all in disorder—naked, in a frightful, obscene nakedness. (Sartre, 1938, pp. 126–127)

When existence is exposed in its full actuality, shorn of words, language and syntax, what comes into view is "monstrous masses". Losing their singularity, their illusory specificity, things turn into formless lumps. This is, in fact, a fascinating paradox: while removing us from the true essence of things, language also is what makes their singularity possible. This is because language is simultaneously the product of separateness and also what makes separateness possible. In the absence of language we cannot distinguish between things and hence fail to perceive their singularity. Sartre, most likely, would argue that singularity itself is a manmade illusion that comes to bestow meaning on a meaningless existence. In the spirit of Lacan, though, we might add that illusion is what inaugurates the human subject: while language drops an entire slice of the Real—it also creates what we experience as inner reality.

Where there is no possibility of generalisation or abstraction it is also impossible to mark rule and exception, or the general and the specific. Everything is equally general and equally specific at one and the same time. This lack of boundary is due to the absence of both inside and outside, of "me" and "not-me". Both definition and divergence from it are impossible. Thus, it is utterly impossible to observe singularity while—also and at the same time—there is nothing but the singular. A thing is only what it is for itself, entertaining no relation to any other thing. Relativity and relation come into being within language, which by its very nature compares, generalises, and marks boundaries. But within the domain of the Real—or the absurd, as Sartre would have called it—things exist without relating and stay external to any relation: they are simultaneously the rule and the absolute exception from any rule.

> All these objects ... how can I explain? They inconvenienced me. [...] I realised that there was no half-way house between non-existence and this flaunting abundance. If you existed, you had to exist *all the way*, as far as mouldiness, bloatedness, obscenity were concerned. (Ibid. pp. 127–128)

Given that distance becomes possible only through language, when the latter is rejected the individual finds him or herself facing an archaic incestuous maternal object, lacking in outline, an object with whom proximity by definition is over-proximity, satiating to the point of nausea, suffocating in its sticky surfeit which fills up all space. It is not just the mother who is prior to language—but the mother against whom language emerges. Language is not merely a testimony to the mother's "negation" and internalisation (Kristeva, 1987a; Green, 1988), but also what allows the child to negate the mother and to distinguish him or herself from her in the first place.

In the absence of a language that enables barriers, the intensity of being within the domain of the Real becomes untenable because of the lack of distance it enforces on the observer. Though distinctions and separations gnaw away at reality, they do make it tolerable. In their absence, existence becomes, in Bion's words, "an undreamable dream"

(Ogden, 2003; Bion, 1962b): a dream that can neither be remembered nor forgotten, neither kept secret nor communicated. It can only be evacuated through hallucinations or delusions, or annihilated through fragmentation or suicide.

Discussion

On the continuum of psychosomatic expressions, metaphoric expression (Lacan's *symptom*) is the most open to interpretation and the richest in contents. More primitive and limited, metonymic expression nevertheless serves, in its slighter way, as a conduit to what remains out of consciousness. The third kind of somatic expression resists not only interpretation but also any type of symbolisation and, thus, denies not only the entire psychic language but the very formation of a "subject within language". This psychosomatic expression does not come to protect the self from psychic contents with which contact is insufferable: its objective is to prevent the formation of a structure that would contain any psychic contents at all. It is a violent refusal of psychic existence, a rejection of the formation of a distinct and distinguishing "I". Such refusal is rooted in the primary experience vis-à-vis a mother the separation from whom was experienced as a catastrophe that cannot be survived.

In practice, we very rarely witness cases in which psychotic psychosomatic expression wholly and totally substitutes symbolic language. But wherever alongside it apparently symbolic language does emerge—it is hollow, mechanical, and empty. Even in personalities that are not fully psychotic we can distinguish, within the psychosomatic phenomenon, a-symbolic zones which guard catastrophic terror regarding separation and separateness as well as an incestuous attraction to a mother individuation from whom is experienced as death.

The name of the father, symbolising legislative and disciplining authority, is the agent whose non-admission can have psychotic consequences, as Malcolm Bowie (2005) claims in his book on Lacan. Within the Symbolic order, it represents all agents who have imposed fixed constraints on the infant's desires, threatening castration by way of punishment for transgression. The name of the father is, in fact, the primary agent of the law, who supplies the chain of signifiers with its mobility as well as its typical reciprocal relations. Once this inaugurating signifier is removed, so is the entire process of signification. The name of the father is the paternal metaphor that powers the whole overarching metaphoric process. It is a crucial anchor for the subject since without it metaphor reaches the subject from the outside, taking the form of hallucinations. Its absence, argues Lacan (2006), leaves a hole in the symbolic universe. The specific agonies to which a person is exposed due to this hole involve an ongoing encounter with the Real—that nevertheless stays totally alien to him or her. Also situated outside the grid of signifiers—it causes uncontrollable upheavals within it.

Psychotic psychosomatic expression is the outcome of a combination of an overwhelming attraction to incestuous fusion with the archaic mother's body and a catastrophic and terminal experience associated with the name of the father. This combination takes us back to the third function of the mother-tongue in the creation of language. It is the function whereby the mother invokes the presence of the father as the one who draws a line between the private and the public and who enables a non-traumatic transition from singular language to plural language, from the first-person to the third-person of experience. To the extent that it is not traumatic, this transition will make it possible for the infant to move between languages and orders in a manner that serves its needs. If, however, the figure of the father is associated with traumatisation, this transition from singular to plural language will be deeply impaired.

The psychotic character of psychosomatic expression will be reflected in its being situated out of the chain of signifiers and the associative grid, namely by being located outside all meaning in a way that negates the subject as the owner of his or her experience and thoughts. Its disintegrating quality on the one hand, and gratifying quality on the other hand—places it in a psychotic domain. One major difference between metaphoric and psychotic psychosomatic expression is that the former includes an organising element, one that manages to gather and hold what is forbidden to thought at a distance from consciousness, and enables consciousness to function relatively fully as a result. Yet, in spite of its success at removing the forbidden contents from thought, metaphoric expression is not entirely satisfying and therefore leaves intact the experience of lack and the desire that constitutes subjectivity and allows for psychic motion. Psychotic psychosomatic expression, by contrast, does not protect the self from falling apart. Rather than being directed against any specific content, it attacks mental life as such. Its destructive power correlates with the intensity of the gratification it supplies, namely with the fact that it reanimates the illusion of fusion with the Real mother, thereby annulling the need to generate psychic motion and psychic language.

There are, thus, physical phenomena that signify, not a repetition of the earliest physical history, but rather a refusal to be separated from the domain in which the body exists, in Ferrari's words, as a concrete original object—prior to the formation of a thinking-reflecting consciousness. This is a rejection of the castration language inflicts, a castration which is essentially bound up with separation from the mother's body and with mourning. It is the inability to make the transition from the Real to the Symbolic without crashing. For the psychotic, the experience of this transition is one of evacuation, loss and disintegration: a loss of connection with reality, a cut which will not heal and after which there will be neither life nor vitality. We may argue that if sticking to the Real is tantamount to the "collapse *of* meaning"—as Kristeva argues in her essay on the "abject" (1982)—for the psychotic individual the connection to the Symbolic constitutes a "collapse *into* meaning". The psychosomatic expression that is the result of this collapse involves neither symbolisation nor conversion, and is, thus, an attack on language rather than a language. The psychosomatic psychotic domain actually rejects any type of differentiation: it refuses generalisations along with their exceptions, declining any attempt to give shape to the sticky, slimy blob of primal matter. At the base of this annihilation is an experience suggesting that the transition from matter to form, from rough and raw chunk to sculpture, from experience to words, cannot be survived.

In the analytic work with psychotic psychosomatic expressions, at times, the analyst him-or-herself may serve as a barrier to chaos. A psychotic transference may occur which essentially resembles the physical experience itself since it opposes any form of separateness (a separateness between inside and outside, in this case, or between reality and fantasy). Within the psychotic transference, clinging to the therapist— much like clinging to the physical phenomenon—is the condition for survival. It is not always the aim of analysis to wean the patient from psychotic transference or from the physical phenomenon itself. Sometimes the latter serves as an "anchor" preventing total collapse. But due to the fragility of the psychotic structure, collapse is at times inevitable. What is required then is the subtle work of naming, the basic and extremely painstaking securing of the various types of differentiation between body and consciousness, between self and other, between experience and thought. The essence of analytic work with psychotic psychosomatic expressions is the construction of a living bridge across the abyss of the undreamable dream—by means of the unshaken presence of the analyst as a speaking body—toward the possibility of dream and language.

Interpretation and over-interpretation

I would like to dedicate this epilogue to one of the most important uses of language. This is the work of interpretation. The tension between interpretation and over-interpretation, or between any work of interpretation that does justice to the object of interpretation and that which lets it slip through the mazes which it opens, this tension actually touches—in different ways—on everything that has been discussed in the foregoing chapters. The question of what we interpret, or for what purpose we interpret, is inextricably bound up, not only with the question of what it is that stands before us, but also with the question concerning the kind of discourse that we create with it. The book that accompanied me in the course of writing this last chapter, so that parts of it came to be interwoven with it throughout, is Joseph Brodsky's *Watermark* (1992).

What is a watermark, in contrast with a usual mark or a stamp? A watermark is a mark that leaves no mark; a mark that is stamped onto transience, onto that which is in constant motion; a mark which is a type of imprint as well as a kind of renunciation. Brodsky's *Watermark* is a unique meditation which the author conducts in the course of forty-eight short chapters, all concerning the city of Venice. They deal with the city in both the physical and the metaphysical sense, and not only with the city as such but rather with its psychic reflections, along with the reflections of the psyche in it.

What do these fragments teach us about the work of interpretation? In her epilogue to her Hebrew translation of Brodsky's book, Leah Dovev presents two quotations. The first is by the Italian author, Italo Calvino, from his novel *Invisible Cities* (1978):

> Dawn had broken when he (Marco Polo) said: 'sire, now I have told you about all the cities I know'.
> 'There is still one of which you never speak'.
> Marco Polo bowed his head.
> 'Venice', the khan said.
> Marco smiled. 'What else do you believe I have been talking to you about?'
> The emperor did not turn a hair. 'And yet I have never heard you mention that name'.
> And Polo said: 'Every time I describe a city I am saying something about Venice.' (Ibid. p. 86)

The second quotation is from the US author Mary McCarthy: "Among Venice's spells is one of peculiar potency: the power to awaken the Philistine dozing in the skeptic's breast." (1956, p. 174)

The work of interpretation, like Venice it would seem, is situated somewhere between these two quotations. It must locate the core that is common to all—that which is the essence of everything so that everything is articulated in relation to it while it is nevertheless in no need of articulation. Simultaneously it must stir into life its opposite principle, the one that challenges and subverts all. The power of interpretation resides more often in its form than in its substance. In the subtle modes of balancing it proposes rather than in the contents of this balance. In the way it "places an object in one's gaze" more than in the actual manner in which it "sees" that object or calls it by a name. It is in this sense that Brodsky, in his book, stakes out an extraordinary interpretive position, one that observes the city's interior and exterior from ever changing distances, filled with wonder yet not losing its humour, fluent yet refusing to give up stuttering, penetrating while not neglecting the representation-reluctant wisdom of surfaces.

Avner Bergstein (2013), an Israeli psychoanalyst, writes:

What the patient internalises is the dreaming function that searches for meaning—not one or another 'specific meaning'. It is the expansion of the psychic container, and not the exposure of unconscious contents, that forms the very core of the analytical process.

I would like to trace here the "dreaming function" of the work of interpretation by means of following fragments from Brodsky's piece and others that communicate with it; fragments each of which illuminates a different dimension of interpretation.

> The eye in this city acquires an autonomy similar to that of a tear. The only difference is that it doesn't sever itself from the body but subordinates it totally. (Brodsky, 1992, p. 44)

What does this sovereignty of the part over the whole, of the organ over the entire body to which it belongs, signify? Each time we are about to interpret we must ask ourselves: What carries what? To what extent is the interpretation we are about to offer, an interpretation which constitutes only a part of the rich, entire thinking body of analysis, actually asserting its rule over the entire analysis? When, moreover, does interpretation expropriate the sovereignty of its interpretative object, and when, rather, does it aim to restore this sovereignty?

The difference between interpretation and over-interpretation never resides in the more or less exact content of the interpretation as such. I would like to assume, for the sake of this discussion, that over-interpretation is not necessarily a misinterpretation. The distinction between correct interpretation and misinterpretation can be discussed in another chapter. The present chapter, however, examines the category of interpretation as opposed to over-interpretation, that is: a category which on the face of it is related not to content but to proportionality in its formal and moral aspects. Yet proportionality is never wholly restricted to form. It is, in itself, content. By this I don't mean that certain interpretations, in terms of their content, come too early or are too revealing. Rather, I argue that the very deviation from the interpretation's aesthetic proportionality is always a professional deviation, hence an ethical one:

> For beauty is where the eye rests. Aesthetic sense is the twin of one's instinct for self preservation and is more reliable than ethics. (Ibid. p. 109)

There, where aesthetic proportionality is right, the eye may rest. Where interpretive proportionality is accurate it will allow the psyche its necessary turning inward, the very movement which interpretation aims to initiate. Interpretation comes neither to take possession nor to occupy. It purports to create a motion of assembling. It is a happening between two people that at its best engenders a happening within one person him-or-herself.

In fact, the notion of the watermark is intended as an oxymoron. One that contains what is inscribed without being inscribed, what is, indeed, written in water, not in the sense of being obliterated or erased, but in the sense of being transient, fluctuating.

Brodsky writes:

> [...] a thought itself possesses a water pattern. So does one's hand-writing; so do one's emotions; so does blood. (Ibid. p. 124)

Perhaps the difference between the language of over-interpretation and the language of interpretation at its best is the same difference between stamp and watermark. What the language of over-interpretation fails to listen to is the transient or mutable. It is a language that clings to rules, reasons, hierarchies, to the order of events and the order of things. How vital, by contrast, is a language that enables space for what cannot be registered—not because of its traumatic qualities but due to its elusiveness, its passing fluidity. Interpretation that does not expropriate its object's sovereignty but actually enables its constitution—is always one that assumes the existence of a part that is not amenable to interpretation, a part that will not let itself be thought through sequence and context or be thought at all. I am not pointing here to the psychotic regions of non-thinking but to a psychic zone to which language-embedded thinking, based as it is on generalisations and assuming generalities, is deeply alien.

A dense, complex, comprehensive interpretation, one that embraces current relations, their roots in the past, the influence of analysis and the early experiences which are re-activated by it—even if substantially correct, may be wrong in the sense of its intentionality. This is the kind of interpretation that puts the truth as its final aim, not the individual. If we are committed to getting a hold on truth, and if we assume that the mind can actually hold truth without changing it by its very holding, then there is some merit in the effort to secure it from the side of the past and the side of the present, from the inside and from the outside. If, however, our interpretation's addressee is the person and not the truth, our offering him or her a rich heavy meal that not only leaves them slightly nauseous but also in a sense shuts them up—is a misguided act of interpretation. An accurate interpretation, in terms of its proportionality, is never stuffing. Quite the contrary: it stirs the appetite.

I would like to illustrate such an interpretation with a fragment taken from Nathan Alterman's play, *Ghosts' Inn* (1974). Three characters—the music-box man, the beggar, and Hananel, are in conversation:

MUSIC-BOX MAN: 'Could we have some silence perhaps? I have to learn this song by heart. I must sing it tomorrow.'

BEGGAR: 'I don't understand. Do you have trouble remembering the words? You yourself composed them.'

MUSIC-BOX MAN: 'I compose them and then again they fall apart.'

BEGGAR: 'That is a sign that you are not composing them properly.'

HANANEL: 'Don't worry. You forget them because you already remember them.' (Ibid. pp. 30–31)

What makes the interpretation that Hananel gives the music-box man so lovely? It's capacity to recognise the anxiety that forgetfulness arouses, but at the same time to recognise the fact that what is forgotten might be forgotten exactly because it has already become engraved in memory; It's capacity to search for reasons but at the same time to turn causality upside down in order to yield meaning.

On water, for instance, you never get absentminded the way you do in the street: your legs keep you and your wits in constant check, as if you were some kind of compass. [...] your sense of the other on water gets keener, as though heightened by a common as well as mutual danger. (Brodsky, 1992, p. 15)

Psychoanalytic sailing, so to speak, involves an increased sense of the other's presence as sharing a joint voyage but on the other hand can also do us harm. One of the biggest questions surrounding the interpretive act is when does it drive its needle deeper—hence allowing it to sketch a wider circle—and when, on the contrary, it unfastens the needle and thereby narrow and limit its radius of movement. An interpretation with the right proportionality obviously includes both of them: it strengthens its hold and broadens the circle. It sustains contact with the ground but as a result allows a rising aloft, or a turning back, or a movement sideways.

Being a vast and fragile sounding box, the analytic setting, to continue the water metaphor, is always already a setting marked by excess: excess sharpness and acuteness; excess reflection. It does not take much for interpretation to become excessive in these terms. Therefore, subtraction is more important to it than addition. And sometimes, I would like to claim, its very strength is in what it leaves out.

> I am not a moral man [...] or a sage. I am neither an aesthete nor a philosopher. I am but a nervous man, by circumstance and by my own deeds. [...] One's eye precedes one's pen, and I resolve not to let my pen lie about its position. Having risked the charge of depravity, I won't wince at that of superficiality either. Surfaces— which is what the eye registers first—are often more telling than their contents, which are provisional by definition [...]. (Ibid. pp. 20–21)

The eye, argues Brodsky, always precedes the pen. In other words: interpretation of a view must never come to conceal this view. And one must even more closely pay attention that the striving for profound meaning won't fall prey to its own greed—to its wish to grab everything, exhaust all, connect all—thus missing the surface whose ripples enfold the element that resists categorisation, perhaps inaccessible to any interpretation at all, the very essence that truly distinguishes one entity from another, one voice from another.

> Inanimate by nature, hotel room mirrors are even further dulled by having seen so many. What they return to you is not your identity but your anonymity [...]. (Ibid. p. 22)

Unlike the mirror, interpretation refracts a person's identity, not his anonymity. But what is the nature of this identity? No experience is more anonymous than the experience of one's psychic biography as nothing but a private instance of a general rule. The therapeutic voyage is never completed by the delineation of the generality of which it is part. Patients are always after that private element which cannot be replaced and which no rule or generalisation will explain or describe. This is the element which will truly be released from anonymity only when the other's gaze will rest on it.

In an article entitled "How love makes the ugly beautiful", Amihud Gilead (2003) argues in a similar context that no beauty exists without a mind to discover, reveal or realise that beauty. It is love that makes singular beings, beauty and necessity or indispensability inseparable (Gilead, 2003, pp. 438, 442). One might, however, also argue the contrary: that the only way to set a person free from his or her anonymity is to leave them, at times, the freedom to be anonymous. To stay, that is, in that Bionian caesural interval in which a pause is the condition for continuation though never ensuring it; in which one stays unknown not because anonymity necessarily leads to the development of identity but because at that moment anonymity is that identity's supreme expression.

> This is the winter light at its purest. It carries no warmth or energy, having shed them and left them behind somewhere in the universe […]. Its particles' only ambition is to reach an object and make it, big or small, visible. It's a private light […]. (Brodsky, 1992, p. 81)

What, then, does this private light consist of?

> A metaphor—or, to put it more broadly, language itself—is by and large open-ended, it craves continuum: an afterlife, if you will. In other words (no pun intended), metaphor is incurable. (Ibid. p. 77)

Like metaphor, interpretation, too, is an essentially open texture which yearns for continuity, which aims for the soul's endurance, not its annihilation. And like metaphor, interpretation is incurable since it creates an opening; since in its purest manifestations it is like a sickness that consumes the body, thus allowing the soul to escape and observe it. I don't refer here to the physical body, not even to the body of feelings, but to the body of language, or to the interpretation's ability to shift from one language to another (whether it is a shift away from the personal language or a shift away from the language of psychoanalysis itself); to the interpretation's ability to allow the transgression of a threshold exactly by means of the recognition of this threshold which cannot be crossed.

> [...] and the answer is that beauty is always external; also, that it is the exception to the rule. (Ibid. p. 108)

Over-interpretation reduces this transgression, while interpretation at its best not only depends on it—but is, itself, an act of transgression.

In his book *Windows*, in a chapter entitled "A flower's name", Pontalis (2000) writes about his aversion to the use (or perhaps, the over-use) of the concept of narcissism:

> So many burdensome words for a short-lived flower, for a worried young man. (2000, p. 39)

This is the crux of what I am trying to say. The word that expropriates the flower; the concept that once again drowns the young man to death.

In her book *The Suppressed Madness of Sane Men* (1987), Marion Milner quotes a saying from the Tao Te Ching, Lao Tse's ancient work:

> It is called mystery.
> Meet it, you cannot see its face;
> Follow it, you cannot see its back. (Milner, 1987, p. 261)

Interpretation may sometimes be the mystery that recognises something without knowing it. That renders something to the gaze without looking at it. I don't mean Winnicott's hidden non-communicative core here—but rather a singular, irreducible and private element which stays silent not because it cannot bear public exposure but because it does not belong to the public and the general, and hence requires a different language, a different way of following it.

In his *Letters to a Young Poet* Rainer Maria Rilke writes:

> [...] for even the best use words wrongly when they want to give them the most delicate and almost inexpressible meaning. But, for all that, I think that you cannot remain without a solution,

if you attach yourself to objects like those with which my eyes are now regaling themselves. If you attach yourself to nature, to the simple and small in her, which hardly anyone sees, but which can so unexpectedly turn into the great and the immeasurable, if you have this love for what is slight and try quite simply as a servant to win the confidence of what appears to you poor, then everything will become easier for you [...].

(Rilke, 1993)

What captivates me in these lines is the advice: "win the confidence". For the interpretive gesture is indeed one that attempts to win the confidence of its object of interpretation. It is the attempt to join the cry, the silence, the refusal, from within.

It is with the following words that Brodsky concludes his book:

The tear is an attempt to remain, to stay behind, to merge [...]. The tear is a throwback, a tribute of the future to the past. Or else it is the result of subtracting the greater from the lesser: beauty from man. (1992, pp. 134–135)

Interpretation, like the tear, "subtracts the greater from the lesser". It is not man, the specific form, which is subtracted from beauty, the general form—but beauty which is subtracted from man. And this is so because it is only when we subtract the general from the individual that we can approach that part of the individual which is not a mere instance of the general; that part of the individual which will never belong to any generality as it will not belong to any other individuality.

When the individual is subtracted from love, love remains as a general form, as the language of the many, as a yearning shared in one way or another by human beings wherever they are. But when love in its general form is subtracted from the individual, what is left is the individual lover in the most purified sense. The interpretation that reveals this purified individuality—or the interpretation that does not quash it in its drive for the truth—is not just interpretation at its best, but probably the only one worth being.

NOTES

Chapter One

1. Although the term "mother tongue" usually refers to the national language of one's birth, here it is used as a concept that refers to the internalised mother's emotional language.
2. Interestingly enough, Bion (1970) once claimed that the stutterer cannot understand his emotions adequately and therefore cannot give them expression in words.

Chapter Two

1. For in fact, being the object at which the discourse is directed, the child serves as a protective barrier against the mother's possible return of repressed material. Its position is both paradoxical and dangerous: while occupying the nearest position to the object of unconscious desire, it must also prevent its return.
2. Paul Celan, Von Schwelle zu Schwelle
   © 1982 Deutsche Verlags-Anstalt, München, in der Verlagsgruppe Random House GmbH.

Chapter Three

1. "An absolute but hidden pact against reality"—Stein, 2005.
2. Much like Ogden (1989) refers to compulsive masturbation as a kind of secondary skin, perversion can be considered as the compulsive production of a shell. The constant excitation resulting from the sense of danger yields an artificial feeling that the various parts of the self are held. This may explain the compulsive repetition: holding disintegrates as soon as satisfaction is achieved. Then the need for the production of a new shell emerges again as the subject faces the fear of disintegration and death.
3. In fact, the entire perverse cycle was re-enacted in the analytic process: from Joel's infiltration of me by means of the literary, artistic language which he knew would appeal to me; to the attempts to inject me with life materials which were then found to be poisonous (see his dream); and to my being "put to death" in the analytic scene which confirmed his primal fantasy about being a source of death.
4. Cristina Comencini, *Don't Tell*, Italy 2005.

Chapter Four

1. Houzel (2004) argues with Tustin on this point, suggesting a more primitive level of bisexuality where masculine elements do not penetrate feminine ones, but simply strengthen the maternal container as a buttress strengthens a building. Houzel emphasises that it is extremely important that the same containing object possesses feminine/maternal and masculine/paternal features in the correct proportions. Any paternal element which is dissociated from the container will be experienced as threatening, persecutory and destructive. The autistic child splits off, very early in life, the component parts of psychic bisexuality, probably because he or she is unable, at that stage, to find enough paternal features in the mother.
2. Music composers do at times use a sustained tone that is not a bass, in a way that is identical to the organ point. When an organ point occurs in a voice other than the bass, it is usually referred to as an "inverted organ point". That is not what I mean here.
3. While the term "syntax" refers to the grammatical structure—the term "semantics", often used in a similar context—refers to the meaning of the vocabulary symbols arranged by that structure. The term "autistic syntax", thus, points to the set of inner rules that determine what is included and excluded from the psychic text. In the case of autistic persons, the syntactic rules are not meant to create a valid meaningful

sentence—but to preserve the sterilisation of language and the evacuation of meaning. It is, therefore, an autistic syntax and not an "autistic semantics".

4. This distinction may also touch upon the difference between autistic and psychotic language. While in psychosis internal rules of action take over—autism is marked by the expropriation of both internal and external rules.

5. Polyphony is any musical text in which two or more tones sound simultaneously (the term derives from the Greek word for "many sounds"). Usually polyphony is associated with counterpoint, the combination of distinct melodic lines. In polyphonic music, two or more simultaneous melodic lines are perceived as independent even though they are related. In the present context—since our thinking, as well as our language and speech, are composed of many different voices, conscious and subconscious, which create texts and subtexts, and since it is the accumulation of all these voices that creates a rich psychic discourse—the attack on psychic polyphony takes place through the creation of a dull discourse that reduces itself to no meaning in order to avoid any encounter with the unbearable.

Chapter Five

1. A "Third" refers to the concrete or imaginary presence of a third person (located out of the primary dyad) that is internalised both as an inner observer and an inner point of view.

2. *Ces Parents Qui Vivent A Travers Moi.*

3. Which Gerson (2004) calls "developmental third".

4. Interestingly, in Hebrew—the language in which this analysis was conducted—one does not speak in the first person but in the "first body". In this sense there was a sort of a double meaning to the "scrap of a body" image.

Chapter Six

1. Bollas's *Hysteria* (1999) also treats the various "conversion experiences" within the texture of self and object relations.

2. Daniel Stern (1985), too, regards language acquisition as a double-edged sword since it severs between two modes of interpersonal experience: experience as such and experience as represented in words. Language, in this sense, permanently fractures the sense of self.

3. "The Words to Say it" (1984).

4. In keeping with Lacan's topography (the Real, the Symbolic etc.) presented in this chapter, "Other" has been capitalised here and refers to Lacan's more structural term, as opposed to a definite singular "other".

5. In the middle of writing these words I took a bite of hot corn on the cob and tears welled up instantaneously. The taste jolted me years back, when I was a child, standing with my mother beside the corn-on-the-cob vendor on the beach. My mother died a few months ago. Before assuming the shape of her face, or the form of my longing—the taste of salty hot corn held something that shrank and crumbled more with every name I attached to it. This is the Real. The taste in its full saltiness, an instant before it becomes a memory. The chasm before it was closed by words.

REFERENCES

Agamben, J. (2009). *What Was Left from Auschwitz*, (Trans: M. Katzir). Tel Aviv: Resling.

Alterman, N. (1974). *Ghosts' Inn*. Tel-Aviv: Hakibutz-Hameuchad.

Alvarez, A. (1980). Two regenerative situations in autism: Reclamation and becoming vertebrate. *Journal of Child Psychotherapy, 6*: 69–80.

Alvarez, A. (1992). *Live Company: Psychotherapy with Autistic, Borderline, Deprived and Abused Children*. London: Routledge.

Amir, D. (2008). *On the Lyricism of the Mind*. Jerusalem and Haifa: Haifa University and Magnes Press.

Anzieu, D. (1987). Some alterations of the ego which make analysis interminable. *International Journal of Psycho-Analysis, 68*: 9–19.

Anzieu, D. (1989). *The Skin Ego*. New Haven, CT, and London: Yale University Press.

Anzieu, D. (1990). *A Skin for Thought, Interviews With Gilbert Tarrab*. London: Karnac.

Aulagnier, P. (2001). *The Violence of Interpretation*, (Trans: Alan Sheridan). London: Routledge.

Bar-On, V. (in press). It cuts both ways: An analysis of the psychological discourse on self injury from a linguistic point of view. *The International Journal of Psychoanalysis*.

147

Baron-Cohen, S. (2003). *The Essential Difference: The Truth about the Male and Female Brain.* NY: Basic Books.

Barrows, P. (2000). The use of stories as autistic objects. Lecture given at The 4th Annual International Frances Tustin Memorial Prize.

Beckett, S. (1953). *Waiting for Godot.* London: Faber and Faber Limited.

Benjamin, J. (1965). Developmental biology in psychoanalysis. In: N. Greenfield & W. Lewis, (Eds.), *Psychoanalysis and Current Biological Thought.* Madison: University of Wisconsin Press.

Benward & Saker (2003). *Music in Theory and Practice, Volume 1.* (7th edn) NY: McGraw Hill College.

Bergstein, A. (2013). Transcending the caesura: reverie, dreaming and counter-dreaming. *International Journal of Psycho-Analysis, 94(4):* 621–644.

Bick, E. (1968). The experience of the skin in early object relations. *International Journal of Psycho-Analysis, 49:* 484–486.

Bick, E. (1986). Further considerations on the function of the skin in early object relations. *British Journal of Psychotherapy, 2(4):* 292–301.

Bion, W. R. (1956). Development of schizophrenic thought. *International Journal of Psycho-Analysis, 37:* 344–346.

Bion, W. R. (1957). Differentiation of the psychotic from the non-psychotic personalities. In: E. B. Spillius (Ed.), *Melanie Klein Today, Volume 1* (pp. 61–78). London and New York: Routledge, 1988.

Bion, W. R. (1959). Attacks on linking. *International Journal of Psycho-Analysis, 40:* 308–315.

Bion, W. R. (1962a). *Learning from Experience.* New York: Basic Books.

Bion, W. R. (1962b). The psycho-analytic study of thinking. *International Journal of Psycho-Analysis, 43:* 306–310.

Bion, W. R. (1962c). A theory of thinking. In: *Second Thoughts.* New York: Jason Aronson.

Bion, W. R. (1962d). *Learning from Experience.* London: Heinmann.

Bion, W. R. (1965). *Transformations: Change from Learning to Growth.* London: Tavistock.

Bion, W. R. (1966). *Catastrophic Change.* Unpublished paper.

Bion, W. R. (1970). *Attention and Interpretation.* London: Tavistock. (1977). Caesura. In: *Two papers: The grid and caesura,* (pp. 35–56). London: Karnac, 1989.

Bollas, C. (1987). *The Shadow of the Object. Psychoanalysis of the Unthought Known.* New York: Columbia University Press. London: Free Association Books.

Bollas, C. (1989). *Forces of Destiny: Psychoanalysis and Human Idiom.* London: Free Association Press.

Bollas, C. (1993). *Being a Character. Psychoanalysis & Self Experience.* London: Routledge.

Bollas, C. (1999). *Hysteria*. New York: Routledge.

Bowie, M. (2005). *Lacan*, (Trans: Judith Goldberg). Tel Aviv: Dvir.

Britton, R. (1993). Fundamentalismus und Idolbildung. In: J. Gutwinski-Jeggle & J. M. Rotmann (eds.). *Die klugen Sinne pflegend: psychoanalytische und kulturkritische Beiträge. Hermann Beland zu Ehren*. Tübingen: Edition Diskord, pp. 100–119.

Britton, R. (1998). Subjectivity, Objectivity and Triangular Space. In: *Belief and Imagination*, (pp. 41–58). London: Routledge, in Association With the Institute of Psychoanalysis.

Brodsky, J. (1992). *Watermark*. New-York: Farrar, Straus and Giroux.

Bromberg, P. M. (1998). *Standing in the Spaces: Essays on Clinical Process, Trauma and Dissociation*. NJ: Analytic Press.

Calvino, I. (1978). *Invisible Cities*, (Trans: William Weaver). London: Harcourt.

Camus, A. (1956). The Fall (La Chute). In: A. Camus, The Plague, The Fall, Exile and the Kingdom, and Selected Essays, (Trans. Justin O'Brien). New York: Everyman's Library, 2004.

Cardinal, M. (1984). *The Words to Say It*, (Trans: Pat Goodheart). Cambride, MA: Van Vactor & Goodheart.

Caruth, C. (1996). *Unclaimed Experience: Trauma Narrative and History*. Baltimore, MD: Johns Hopkins University Press.

Celan, P. (1959). Language mesh, (Trans: Michael Hamburger): donnafleischer.wordpress.com/2010/08/05/paul-celan-language-mesh-sprachgitter/.

Celan, P. (1995). "Speak you too". In: Felstiner, J. (1995). *Paul Celan: Poet, Survivor, Jew*, (pp. 79–81). New Haven and London: Yale University Press.

Chasseguet-Smirgel, J. (1984). *Creativity and Perversion*. London: Routledge.

Corbett, K. (2001). More life: centrality and marginality in human development. *Psychoanalytic Dialogues, 11*: 313–335.

Corbett, K. (2008). Gender now. *Psychoanalytic Dialogues, 18*: 838–856.

Dimen, M. (2001). Perversion is us? Eight notes. *Psychoanalytic Dialogues, 11*: 825–860.

Dorey, R. (1986). The relationship of mastery. *International Review of Psycho-Analysis, 13*: 323–332.

Durban, J. (2002). On love, hatred and anxiety—an introduction to Kleinian thinking. In: *Melanie Klein—Selected Writings*. Tel-Aviv: Bookworn Publishers.

Durban, J. (2011). Shadows, ghosts and chimaeras: On some early modes of handling psycho-genetic heritage. *International Journal of Psycho-Analysis, 92*: 903–924.

Efrati, D. & Israeli, Y. (2007). *The Philosophy and Psychoanalysis of Jacques Lacan*. Israel: Ministry of Defense Publishing House.

Eshel, O. (1998). Black holes, deadness and existing analytically. *International Journal of Psycho-Analysis, 79*: 1115–1130.

Eshel, O. (2005). Pentheus rather than Oedipus: On perversion, survival and analytic "presencing". *International Journal of Psycho-Analysis, 86*: 1071–1097.

Felman, S. & Laub, D. (1992). *Testimony: Crises of Witnessing in Literature, Psychoanalysis, and History.* New York and London: Routlegde.

Ferenczi, S. (1932). *The Clinical Diary.* Judith Dupont (Ed.). Cambridge & London: Harvard University Press, 1988.

Ferenczi, S., Abraham, K., Simmel, E., & Jones, E. (1921). *Psychoanalysis of the War Neurosis.* London: International Psychoanalysis Press.

Ferrari, A. B. (2004). *From the Eclipse of the Body to the Dawn of Thought.* London: Free Association Books.

Fonagy, P. (2001). *Attachment Theory and Psychoanalysis.* New York: Other Press.

Fonagy, P., Gergely, G., Jurist, E. L., & Target, M. (2002). *Affect Regulation, Mentalization, and the Development of the Self.* New York: Other Press.

Frank, R. J. (2000). *Non-Chord Tones, Theory on the Web.* Dallas: Southern Methodist University Press.

Freud, S. (1905d). *Three Essays on the Theory of Sexuality. S. E., 7,* (pp. 136–248). London: Hogarth.

Freud, S. (1919e). A child is being beaten: A contribution to the study of the origin of sexual perversions. *S. E., 17,* (pp. 179–204). London: Hogarth.

Freud, S. (1920g). *Beyond the Pleasure Principle, S. E., 18,* (pp. 3–64). London: Hogarth.

Freud, S. (1922b). Some neurotic mechanisms in jealousy, paranoia and homosexuality. *S. E., 18,* (pp. 221–233). London: Hogarth.

Freud S. (1923b). *The Ego and the Id. S. E., 19.* London: Hogarth.

Freud, S. (1923e). The infantile genital organization: An interpolation into the theory of sexuality. *S. E., 19,* (pp. 141–148). London: Hogarth.

Freud, S. (1927e). *Fetishism. S. E., 21,* (pp. 152–159). London: Hogarth.

Freud, S. (1930a [1929]). *Civilization and its Discontents. S. E., 21,* (pp. 64–148). London: Hogarth.

Freud, S. (1940e [1938]). Splitting of the ego in the process of defense. *S. E., 23,* (pp. 8–271). London: Hogarth.

Freud, S. (1950a [1887–1902]). Project for a scientific psychology. *S. E., 1,* (pp. 281–391). London: Hogarth.

Freud, S. & Breuer, J. (1895d [1893–1895]). *Studies on Hysteria. S. E., 2,* (pp. 1–323). London: Hogarth.

Gaddini, E. (1969). On imitation. *International Journal of Psycho-analysis, 50*: 475–484.

Gampel, Y. (1999). Between the background of safety and the background of the uncanny in the context of social violence. In: E. Bott Spillius (Ed.), *Psychoanalysis on the Move*, (pp. 59–74). London: Routledge.

Gampel, G. (2005). Presence: A developmental perspective: Foreword. In: Alvarez, A., *Live Company: Psychotherapy with Autistic, Borderline, Deprived and Abused Children*, (Trans: Ora Zilberstein). Tel-Aviv: Bookworm.

Gampel, Y. (2010). *Ces parents qui vivent à travers moi*. Trans: Mishor, T. Jerusalem: Keter.

Ghent, E. (1990). Masochism, submission, surrender—masochism as a perversion of surrender. *Contemporary Psychoanalysis, 26*: 108–136.

Gilead, A. (2003). How does love make the ugly beautiful? *Philosophy and Literature, 27*(2): 436–443.

Glasser, M. (1986). Identification and its vicissitudes as observed in the perversions. *International Journal of Psycho-Analysis, 67*: 9–16.

Glover, E. (1933). The relation of perversion-formation to the development of reality-sense. *International Journal of Psycho-Analysis, 14*: 486–504.

Green, A. (1988). The primordial mind and the work of the negative. *International Journal of Psycho-Analysis, 79*: 649–665.

Grotstein, J. (1980). A proposed revision of the psychoanalytic concept of primitive mental states: 1. An introduction to a newer psychoanalytic metapsychology. *Contemporary Psychoanalysis, 16*(4): 479–546.

Grotstein, J. S. (1990a). Nothingness, meaninglessness, chaos and the "black hole": The importance of nothingness, meaninglessness and chaos in psychoanalysis. *Contemporary Psychoanalysis, 26*: 257–290.

Grotstein, J. S. (1990b). The "black hole" as the basic psychotic experience. *Journal of the American Academy of Psychoanalysis, 18*: 29–46.

Grotstein, J. S. (2000). *Who is the Dreamer, Who Dreams the Dream?* NJ and London: The Analytic Press.

Hamilton, V. (1992). The protective shell in children and adults. *International Journal of Psycho-Analysis, 73*: 173–176.

Harris, A. E. (2011). Gender as a strange attractor: Discussion of the transgender symposium. *Psychoanalytic Dialogues, 21*: 230–238.

Hartmann, H. (1939 [1958]). *Ego Psychology and the Problems of Adaptation*. New York: International Universities Press.

Hartmann, H. (1953 [1964]). *Contribution to the Meta-psychology of Schizophrenia, Essays on Ego Psychology*, (pp. 182–206). New York: International Universities Press.

Hermann, I. (1976). Clinging—going-in-search—a contrasting pair of instincts and their relation to sadism and masochism [1935]. *The Psychoanalytic Quarterly, 45*: 5–36.

Horesh, G. (2006). Thoughts on Corporeality. A lecture given at the Israeli Psychoanalytic Society.

Houzel, D. (2004). The psychoanalysis of infantile autism:1. *Journal of Child Psychotherapy, 30*: 225–237.

Iacoboni, M. Woods, R. P., Brass, M., Bekkering, H., Mazziotta, J. C., & Rizzolatti, G. (1999). Cortical mechanisms of human imitation, *Science, 286(5449)*: 2526–2528.

Jacobson, R. (1956). Two aspects of language and two types of aphasic disturbances. In: Jacobson, R. (1971). *Selected Writings—Word and Language, Volume 2*, (pp. 239–259). Den-Haag—Paris: Mouton .

Joseph, B. (1971). A clinical contribution to the analysis of a perversion. *International Journal of Psycho-Analysis, 52*: 441–449.

Keinan, N. (2007). The hollowed envelope—the therapeutic work with 'holes' in the psyche. Lecture given at the Psychoanalytic Israeli Society.

Kernberg, O. (1995). *Aggression in Personality Disorders and Perversions*. New Haven: Yale University Press.

Khan, M. R. (1964). Ego distortion, cumulative trauma, and the role of reconstruction in the analytic situation. *International Journal of Psycho-Analysis, 45*: 272–279.

Khan, M. R. (1979). *Alienation in Perversions*. New York: International Universities Press.

Klein, M. (1923). The development of a child. *International Journal of Psychoanalysis, 4*: 419–474.

Klein, M. (1952). Some theoretical conclusions regarding the emotional life of the infant. In: *Developments in Psycho-analysis with Heimann, Issacs and Riviere*. London: Hogarth.

Kohut, H. (1971). *The Analysis of the Self*. New York: International Universities Press.

Kohut, H. (1972). Lecture 1 (January 7, 1972): Perversions. In: P. Tolpin & M Tolpin (eds.). *The Chicago Institute lectures*, (pp. 1–11). Hillsdale, NJ: Analytic Press, 1996.

Kohut, H. (1977). *The Restoration of the Self*. New York: International Universities Press.

Kristeva, J. (1982). Powers of Horror: An Essay on Abjection, (Trans: Leon S. Roudiez). Columbia University Press.

Kristeva, J. (1987a). *Black Sun: Depression and Melancholia*, (Trans: Leon S. Roudiez). New-York: Columbia University Press.

Kristeva, J. (1987b). Tales of Love. New York: Columbia University Press.

Kristeva, J. (1995). *New Maladies of the Soul*, (Trans: Ross Guberman). New York: Columbia University Press.

Lacan, J. (1958). *Écrits*, (Trans: Bruce Fink). London: W. W. Norton, 2007.

Lacan, J. (2006). *On the Names of the Father*, (Trans: Noam Baruch). Tel-Aviv: Resling.

Lao Tze (c. 600 BC) *Tao Te Ching*, (Trans: Ch'u Ta Kao 1937). London: Buddhist Society.

Laplanche, J. & Pontalis, J. -B. (2004). *Fantasme originaire, Fantasmes des origine, Origine du fantasme*, (Trans: Davidson, G). Tel Aviv: Resling.

Laub, D. (2005). Traumatic shutdown of narrative and symbolization. *Contemporary Psycho-analysis, 41*: 307–326.

Liska, V. (2009). After the silence: holocaust remembrance in contemporary Austrian-Jewish literature. In: *When Kafka Says We: Uncommon Communities in German-Jewish Literature*, (pp. 151–159). Bloomington and Indianapolis: Indiana University Press.

Maiello, S. (1995). The sound-object: A hypothesis about prenatal auditory experience and memory. *Journal of Child Psychotherapy, 21*: 23–41.

Manicia, M. (1981). On the beginning of mental life in the foetus. *International Journal of Psycho-Analysis, 62*: 351–357.

Matte-Blanco, I. (1975). *The Unconscious as Infinite Sets*. London: Duckworth.

McCarthy, M. (1956). *Venice Observed*. London: Heinmann.

McDougall, J. (1978). The Primal Scene and Perverse Scenario. In: *Plea for a Measure of Abnormality*, (pp. 53–86). New York: International Universe Press, 1980.

McDougall, J. (1982). *Théâtres du Je*. Paris: Gallimard.

McDougall, J. (1989). *Theatres of the Body*. London: Free Association Books.

Meltzer, D. (1992). *The Claustrum—An Investigation of Claustrophobic Phenomena*. Pertshire, UK: Clunie Press.

Meltzer, D., & Harris-Williams, M. (1988). Holding the dream. In: *The Apprehension of Beauty*, (pp: 178–199). Scotland: Clunie Press.

Meltzer, D., Bremner, J., Hoxter, S., Weddel D. & Wittenberg, I. (1975). *Explorations in Autism*. Pertshire, UK: Clunie Press.

Milner, M. (1987). *The Suppressed Madness of Sane Men: Forty-four Years of Exploring Psychoanalysis*. New Library of Psychoanalysis, 3: 1–297. London and New York: Tavistock Publications.

Mitchell, S. A. (1997). Psychoanalysis and the degradation of romance. *Psychoanalytic Dialogues, 7*: 23–41.

Mitchell, S. A. (2000). *Relationality: From Attachment to Intersubjectivity*. Hillsdale, NJ: The Analytic Press.

Mitrani, J. (1992). On the survival function of autistic maneuvers In adult patients. *International Journal of Psychoanalysis, 73*(2): 549–560.

Mitrani, J. (1994). On adhesive-pseudo-object relations: Part 1—theory. *Contemporary Psychoanalysis, 30*(2): 348–366.

Mitrani, J. L. (1995). Toward an understanding of unmentalized experience. *Psychoanalitic Quarterly, 64*: 68–112.

Mitrani, J. (2009). The problem of empathy: Bridging the gap between neuroscience and psychoanalysis toward understanding autism. *Fort Da, 15*: 7–32.

Moore, R. (1999). *The Creation of Reality in Psychoanalysis.* Hillsdale, NJ: The Analytic Press.

Ogden, T. (1986). *The Matrix of the Mind.* Northvale, NJ: Jason Aronson.

Ogden, T. (1989a). The autistic-contiguous position. In: *The Primitive Edge of Experience.* Northvale, N.J: Jason Aronson.

Ogden, T. H. (1989b). *The Primitive Edge of Experience.* Northvale, NJ: Jason Aronson; London: Karnac.

Ogden, T. H. (1999). The perverse subject of analysis. In: *Reverie and Interpretation: Sensing Something Human,* (pp. 65–104). Northvale, NJ: Jason Aronson.

Ogden T. (2001). Re-minding the body. In: *Conversations at the Frontier of Dreaming,* (pp. 153–174). London: Karnac.

Ogden, T. (2003). On not being able to dream. *International Journal of Psycho-Analysis, 84*: 17–30.

Oliner, M. (1996). External reality: The elusive dimensions of psychoanalysis. *Psychoanalitic Quarterly, 65*: 267–300.

Pantone, P. J. (2004). The growing consensus in developmental theory. *Contemporary Psychoanalysis, 40*: 310–315.

Parsons, M. (2000). Sexuality and perversion: A hundred years on. *International Journal of Psycho-Analysis, 81*: 37–49.

Pontalis, J. -B. (1980). *Perdre de vue.* Paris: Gallimard.

Pontalis, J. -B. (2000). *Windows,* (Trans: Orit Rosen). Tel-Aviv: Bookworm.

Ramachandran, V. S. & Oberman, L. M. (2006). Broken mirrors: a theory of autism. *Scientific American, November*: 63–69.

Rayner, E. (1981). Infinite experiences, affects and the characteristics of the unconscious. *International Journal of Psycho-Analysis, 62*: 403–412.

Reich, W. (1949). *Character Analysis.* New York: Farrar, Straus & Giroux.

Reick, M. (2011). Body of knowledge. A lecture given at the Israeli Psychoanalytic Society.

Ricks, D. (1975). Vocal communication in pre-verbal, normal and autistic children. In: N. O'Connor (Ed.), *Language, Cognitive Defects and Retardation.* London: Butterworths.

Rilke, R. M. (1992). *The Notebooks of Malte Laurids Brigge,* (Trans: M. D. Herter). New York: Norton.

Rilke, R. M. (1993). *Letters to a Young Poet,* (Trans: M. D. Herter). New York: Norton.

Rilke, R. M. (2000). *The Duino Elegies.* (Trans: John Waterfield). New York: Edwin Mellen Press.

Rizzolatti, G. et al. (1996). Premotor cortex and the recognition of motor actions. *Cognitive Brain Research, 3*: 131–141.

Sandler, J. (1960). The background of safety. *International Journal of Psycho-Analysis, 41*: 352–365.

Sartre, P. (1938). *Nausea.* (Trans: Lloyd Alexander). New-York: A New Direction Paperbook, 2007.

Schellekes, A. (2008). The dread of falling and dissolving: Further thoughts. Lecture given at The 12th Annual International Frances Tustin Memorial Prize.

Stein, R. (1999). The entitlement of the object in perversion. Paper presented at Freud at the Threshold of the twentieth-century conference. The Freud Center, Hebrew University, Jerusalem.

Stein, R. (2003). Why perversion?—Paper presented on the IARPP Online Colloquium, November.

Stein, R. (2005). Why perversion? "False love" and the perverse pact. *International Journal of Psycho-Analysis, 86*: 775–799.

Stern, D. (1985). *The Interpersonal World of the Infant.* New-York: Basic Books.

Stevens, W. (1923). *Harmonium.* New York: Alfred A. Knopf, September 7: 24. York University Library Special Collections 734.

Stoller, R. J. (1974). Hostility and mystery in perversion. *International Journal of Psycho-Analysis, 55*: 425–434.

Stoller, R. J. (1975). *Perversion: The Erotic Form of Hatred.* New York: Pantheon Books.

Stoller, R. J. (1991). *Pain and Passion: A Psychoanalyst Explores the World of S and M.* New York: Plenum.

Sullivan, H. S. (1953). *The Interpersonal Theory of Psychiatry.* New York: Norton.

Troisier, H. (1998). *Piera Aulagnier.* Tel-Aviv: Bookworm.

Tustin, F. (1981). *Autistic States in Children.* London: Routledge & Kegan Paul Ltd.

Tustin, F. (1986). *Autistic Barriers in Neurotic Patients.* London: Karnac.

Tustin, F. (1988). The "black hole"—a significant element in autism. *Free Association, 11*: 35–50.

Tustin, F. (1990). *The Protective Shell in Children and Adults.* London: Karnac.

Van der Kolk, B., McFarlane, A. & Weisaeth, L. (1996). *Traumatic Stress: The Effects of Overwhelming Experience on Mind, Body, and Society.* New York: The Guilford Press.

Vanier, A. (2003). *Lacan,* (Trans: Squverer Amos). Tel-Aviv: Resling.

Winnicott, D. W. (1949). Mind and its relation to the psyche-soma. In: *Through Pediatrics to Psychoanalysis,* (pp. 243–254). London: Hogarth Press.

Winnicott, D. W. (1953). Transitional objects and transitional phenomena—a study of the first "not-me" possession. *International Journal of Psycho-Analysis, 34*: 89–97.

Winnicott, D. W. (1958). Transitional objects and transitional phenomena. In: *Collected Papers. Through Pediatrics to Psychoanalysis*. London: Tavistok Publications.

Winnicott, D. W. (1960a). Ego distortion in terms true and false self. In: *The Maturational Processes and the Facilitating Environment: Studies in the Theory of Emotional Development*, (pp. 140–151). London: Hogarth Press.

Winnicott, D. W. (1960b). The theory of the parent-infant relationship. In: *The Maturational Processes and the Facilitating Environment: Studies in the Theory of Emotional Development*. London: Hogarth Press.

Winnicott, D. W. (1965). A clinical study of the effect of a failure of the average expectable environment on a child's mental functioning. *International Journal of Psycho-Analysis, 46*: 81–87.

Wiseman, H. & Barber, J. P. (2008). *Echoes of the Trauma: Relational Themes and Emotions in Children of Holocaust Survivors*. Cambridge: Cambridge University Press.

INDEX